AF413196

Esther Mahlangu

HANDBOOK

text by

LARRY OSSEI-MENSAH

edited by

LARRY WARSH

NO MORE RULERS

In association with No More Rulers
nomorerulers.com @nomorerulers

NO MORE RULERS ®

The NO MORE RULERS mark and logo are registered trademarks
of No More Rulers, Inc.

ISBN: 979-8-9889286-3-8

Design by Hannah Alderfer, HHAdesign

This book has been composed in Helvetica Neue Pro

Printed on acid-free paper

Printed in China

Front cover:
Untitled (Ndebele Abstract), 2019
Acrylic paint on canvas
41 1/3 inches (105 cm) in diameter

CONTENTS

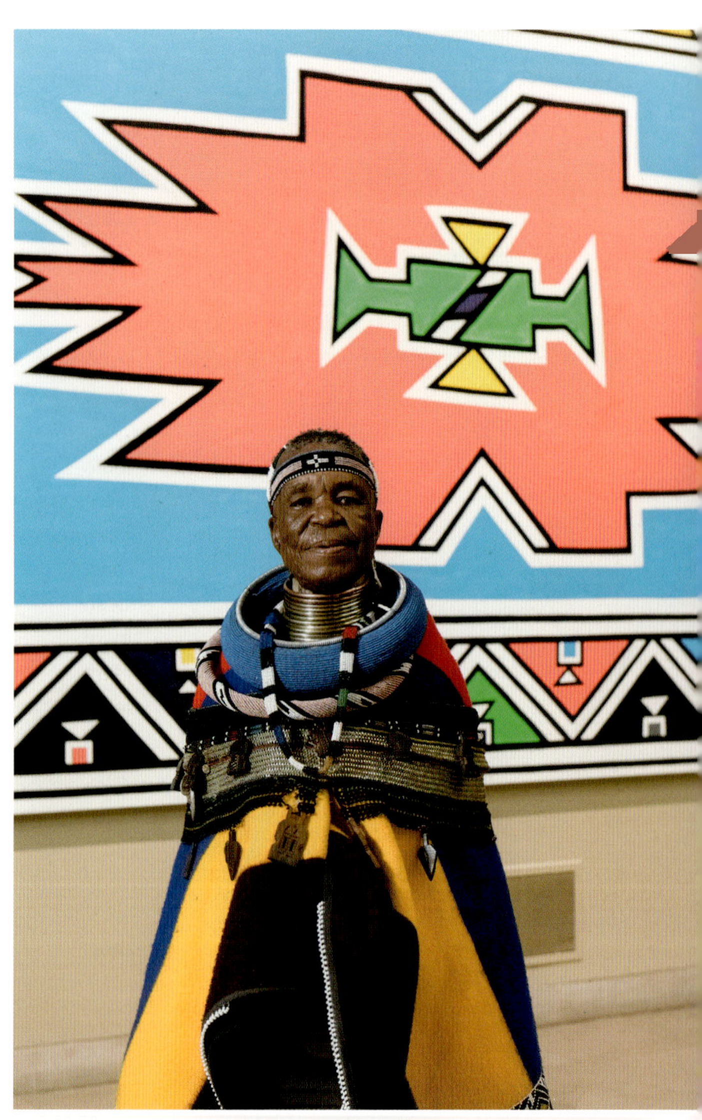

Esther Mahlangu, 2014

FOREWORD

The world has changed enormously since I first became enamored with Esther Mahlangu's art in 1989, when I saw it in the exhibition *Magiciens de la Terre* at the Centre Pompidou in Paris. I've changed a bit myself since then, but my interest in Mahlangu and her work remains a constant in my life as her stature in the international art world continues to grow. Recently Mahlangu has been acknowledged with a major retrospective in her home country of South Africa, and her work is gaining even more audiences globally. Seeing her art on view at the Brooklyn Museum, the Serpentine Gallery in London, and the Louvre Abu Dhabi, among other institutions, is a great pleasure. In the US, her work has been collected by the Los Angeles County Museum of Art (LACMA), the Hirshhorn Museum and Sculpture Garden in Washington, DC, the Pérez Art Museum Miami, and the Brooklyn Museum, to name a few, and acquisitions are in process at other museums. That, too, is a great pleasure to see.

Mahlangu's work also speaks to an audience beyond the museum and gallery circuit. Her venturesome spirit is reflected in a willingness to consider almost any surface as a canvas for her art—from her first painted BMW car in 1991 to skateboard decks, vases, and the hard hats worn by miners in her home district in northeastern South Africa. She is generously open to collaboration, having worked with everyone from minimalist master Sol LeWitt to music icon John Legend, her collaborator in a design for an international vodka brand.

A remarkable thing about Mahlangu's art is that it is effective at every scale, from small, intimate canvases to designs that cover entire buildings. I have a special affinity for Mahlangu's large-scale public artworks. That includes the murals on canvas she painted for the Virginia Museum of Fine Arts in 2014, which since then have been welcoming visitors to the museum's African art galleries. Grounded in the wall-painting traditions of her people, the Ndebele, Mahlangu's geometric abstractions interact with architecture to dynamically energize public spaces.

Born in 1935, Mahlangu is a role model for every generation, not only in South Africa but globally. She is a strong woman who has endured many hardships. Throughout her life, she has maintained a strong sense of identity, spiritually and visually. To me, she is a national treasure for South Africa, and for the world. "I love art. It is part of me," she has said. "I will continue to paint as long as I am able."

With that in mind, my goal with this handbook is to introduce Mahlangu as an international artist. The *Esther Mahlangu Handbook* is a guide for new audiences and for those looking to deepen their understanding of this exceptional artist and her work. Written by curator Larry Ossei-Mensah, the text starts by educating us in the traditional art of the Ndebele people, the better to appreciate how Mahlangu uses those visual traditions as the springboard for her own uniquely contemporary art. As with all books in the *Handbook* series, I invite you to immerse yourself in Mahlangu's creativity, and perhaps inspire your own.

Larry Warsh
New York City
2025

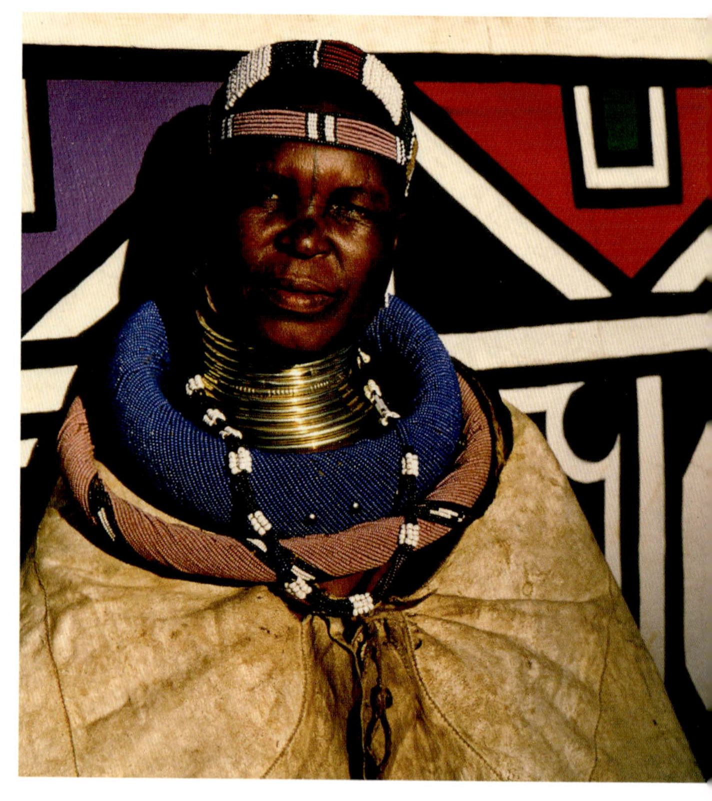

Esther Mahlangu, 1979

INTRODUCTION
WHO IS ESTHER MAHLANGU?

Dr. Esther Mahlangu—affectionately known as Mam' Esther—is a revered South African artist celebrated globally for her vivid paintings, murals, and three-dimensional works filled with bold geometric forms and striking colors. This handbook delves into her vibrant life and extraordinary artistry, exploring the varying elements of Mahlangu's legendary career. These elements are deeply rooted in the rich traditions of her people, the Ndebele of South Africa's northeastern region. Mahlangu first gained international prominence in 1989 as part of a group exhibition at the Centre Georges Pompidou in Paris. Since then, she has become increasingly known for her museum and gallery exhibitions, innovative collaborations, and high-profile projects. The *Esther Mahlangu Handbook* introduces Mahlangu's artistic legacy by exploring the nuances of her work, her role in contemporary art, and her profound engagement with the cultural heritage that has shaped her creative practice.

Esther Mahlangu's work represents a vital intersection between traditional and contemporary art, creating a visual language that bridges her heritage and the international art world. She does not merely replicate tradition but reimagines and innovates within her own creative framework, challenging the Western-centric narratives that have historically marginalized Indigenous and African artists in contemporary art discourses. Her work expands the international art narrative, implicitly arguing for greater inclusion and recognition of art forms from across the global South. This is especially significant given the historical context of colonial oppression and suppression, which has often sought to erase Indigenous identities, rituals, and practices.

As an educator and cultural advocate, Esther Mahlangu has inspired individuals, communities, and other artists to engage meaningfully with their cultural heritages. Her collaborations with global institutions and brands highlight traditional art's dynamic and evolving nature, underscoring its relevance and adaptability in contemporary contexts. In every piece she creates, Mahlangu offers a compelling personal perspective that emphasizes the importance of cultural preservation while showcasing the power of art to engage audiences worldwide.

Born in 1935 in Middelburg, a town in Mpumalanga province in northeastern South Africa, Esther

Originally installed at Mahlangu's homestead, this sign was shown at the Iziko South African National Museum, Cape Town, as part of the 2024 exhibition *Then I knew I was good at painting: Esther Mahlangu, a Retrospective*. Mahlangu was the first woman of her community to travel overseas, flying to Paris for the 1989 exhibition *Magicienes de la Terre*.

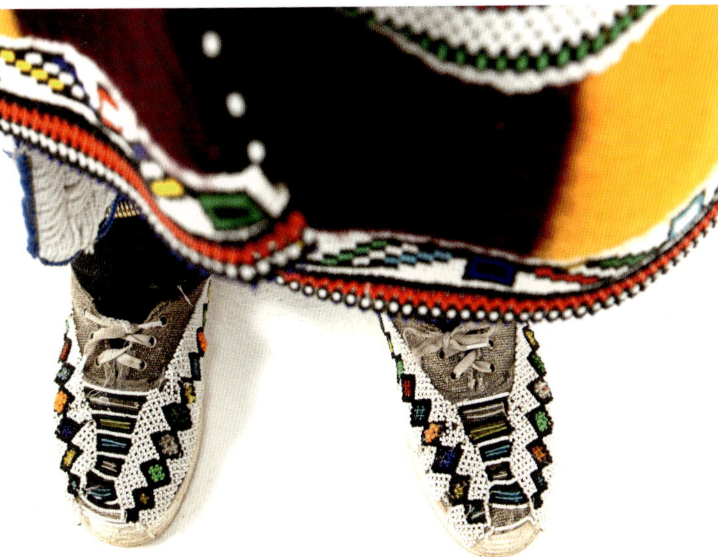

Mahlangu was the eldest of nine children. Growing up in a traditional Ndebele household, cultural practices were an integral part of her daily life, reflected in everything from the architecture of her home to the elaborate beadwork adorning traditional garments. Under the tutelage of her mother and grandmother, Mahlangu mastered the intricate techniques of Ndebele wall and house painting. After starting at the back of the building, out of public view, she was finally invited to join the women in painting the front. In Ndebele culture, wall painting is exclusively women's work, with women adorning their homes with elaborate patterns and designs closely linked to beadwork, another Ndebele art form done by women.

Esther Mahlangu dressed in traditional Ndebele attire, 2018

"When a married Ndebele woman, dressed in full beaded adornment, walks in front of the painted walls of her home, you can see they are one. All her colors and shapes talk to one another."

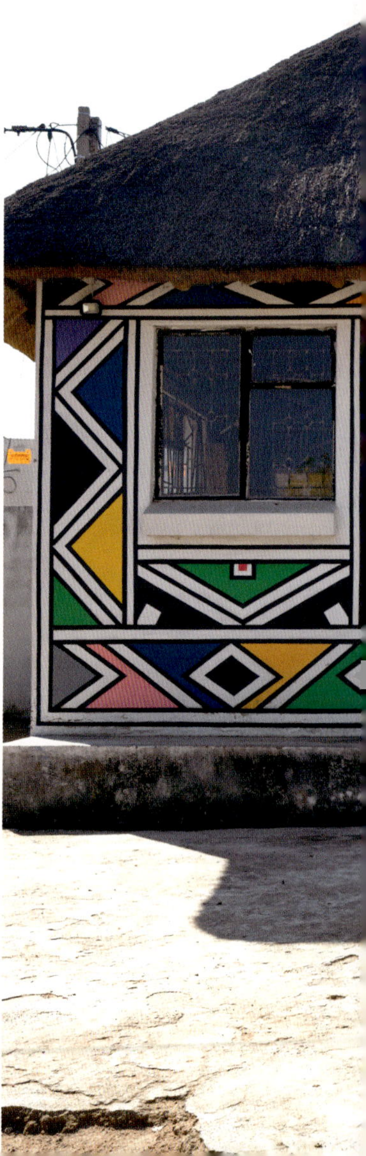

Mahlangu outside one of the buildings at her homestead in Mpumalanga, South Africa, 2023

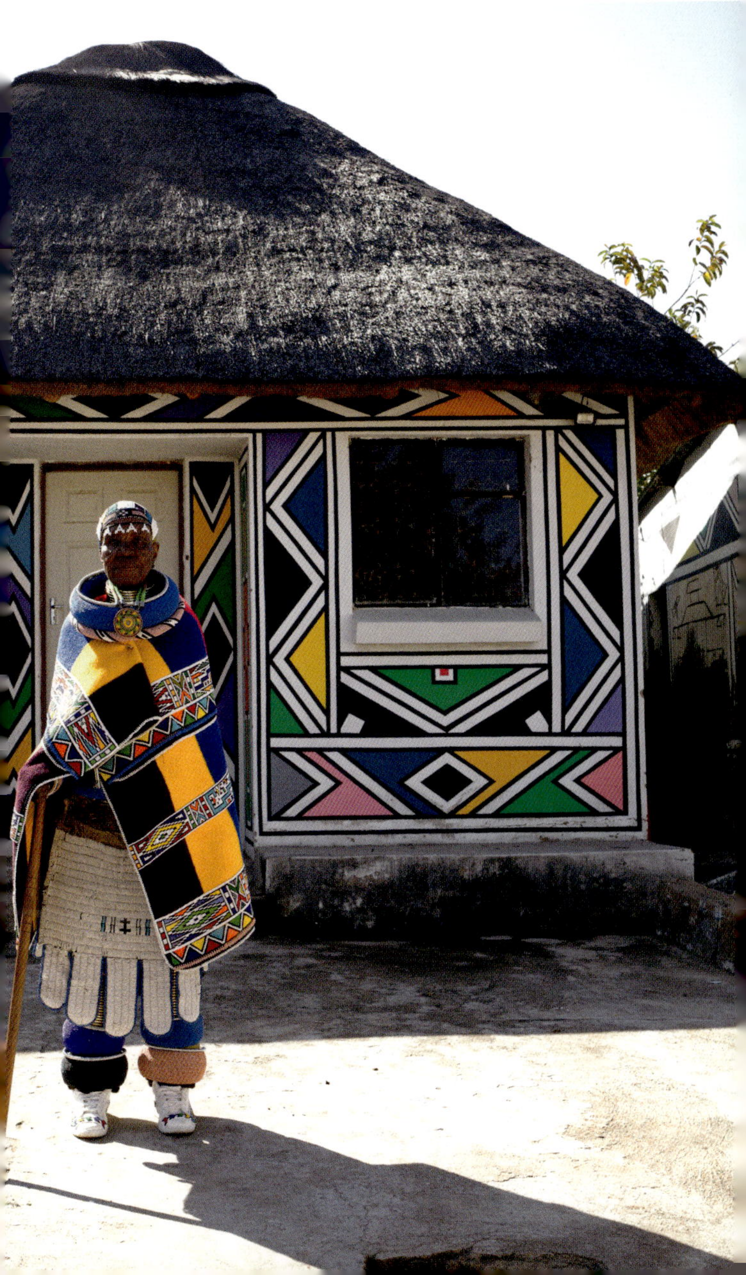

Wall painting has often served as a rite of passage for Ndebele women. Mahlangu has remarked, "When a married Ndebele woman, dressed in full beaded adornment, walks in front of the painted walls of her home, you can see they are one. All her colors and shapes talk to one another."[1] As a girl, Mahlangu learned to create paints from natural pigments and apply them precisely to a variety of different surfaces, using chicken feathers and bundled sticks as brushes. These methods required a steady hand, a keen eye for detail, and a profound understanding of the symbolic language embedded in the patterns.

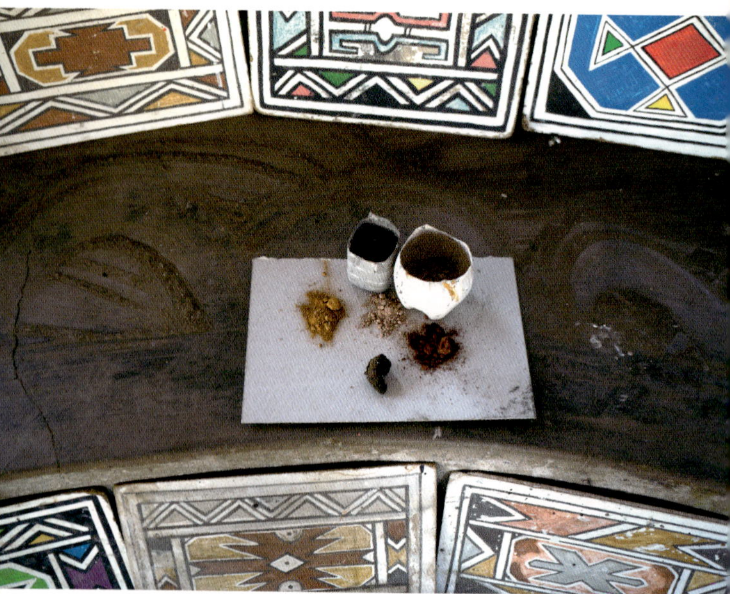

Natural pigments traditionally used for painting, with works by Mahlangu made using natural pigments and acrylic paints, Mpumalanga, South Africa, 2023

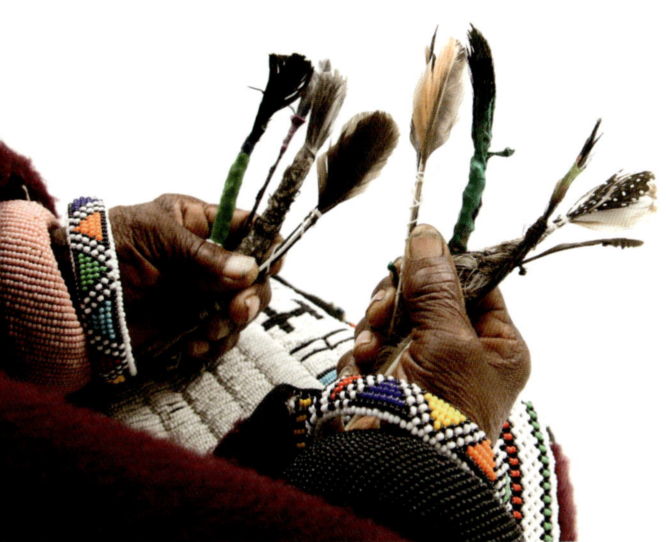

Ndebele wall painting as an art practice underwent significant evolution during the Dutch colonial occupation. After their defeat by Dutch (Boer) settlers in 1883, the Ndebele people faced displacement and severe oppression. In response, homebuilding and wall painting took on new roles as powerful forms of resistance, articulating Ndebele cultural resilience and helping the community establish a sense of place and presence amid adversity. During this period, mud-walled houses became the predominant architectural form, providing an expansive canvas for artistic, cultural, and personal expression. Ndebele artists developed a sophisticated coded language in which patterns and symbols communicated messages of unity, endurance, and the preservation of cultural heritage.

Mahlangu holding brushes made from chicken feathers, 2018. As a child, she learned to paint using brushes like these.

This quiet defiance was a potent form of resistance against the erasure of their identity. Growing up in 1940s South Africa during the rise of Apartheid, young Esther Mahlangu absorbed these lessons deeply, grounding her artistic expression in her people's enduring strength and resilience.

Amid this social and political upheaval, Mahlangu's commitment to her artistic practice became part of that spirit of defiance, mirroring the actions of the elder Ndebele women around her. These women preserved the Ndebele people's sense of identity through wall painting, asserting their space in an increasingly hostile environment. Maintaining various forms of artistic expression, Ndebele women contributed to their community's tenacity, continuity, and cohesion amid severe external pressures and challenges. Her formative years in this resistance environment laid the foundation for Mahlangu's lifelong commitment to using her art as a source of strength, joy, and cultural affirmation.

In 1980, as a married woman with a family of her own, Esther Mahlangu embarked on a significant chapter of her life by becoming an artist-educator at the Botshabelo Museum—an open-air museum near Middelburg dedicated to presenting and preserving Ndebele culture. During more than a decade at the museum, Mahlangu gained valuable insights into the role of cultural institutions as platforms for creative exchange, dialogue, discovery, and education. This experience deepened her

Esther Mahlangu teaching a young student in Mabhoko, Mpumalanga, South Africa, 1992

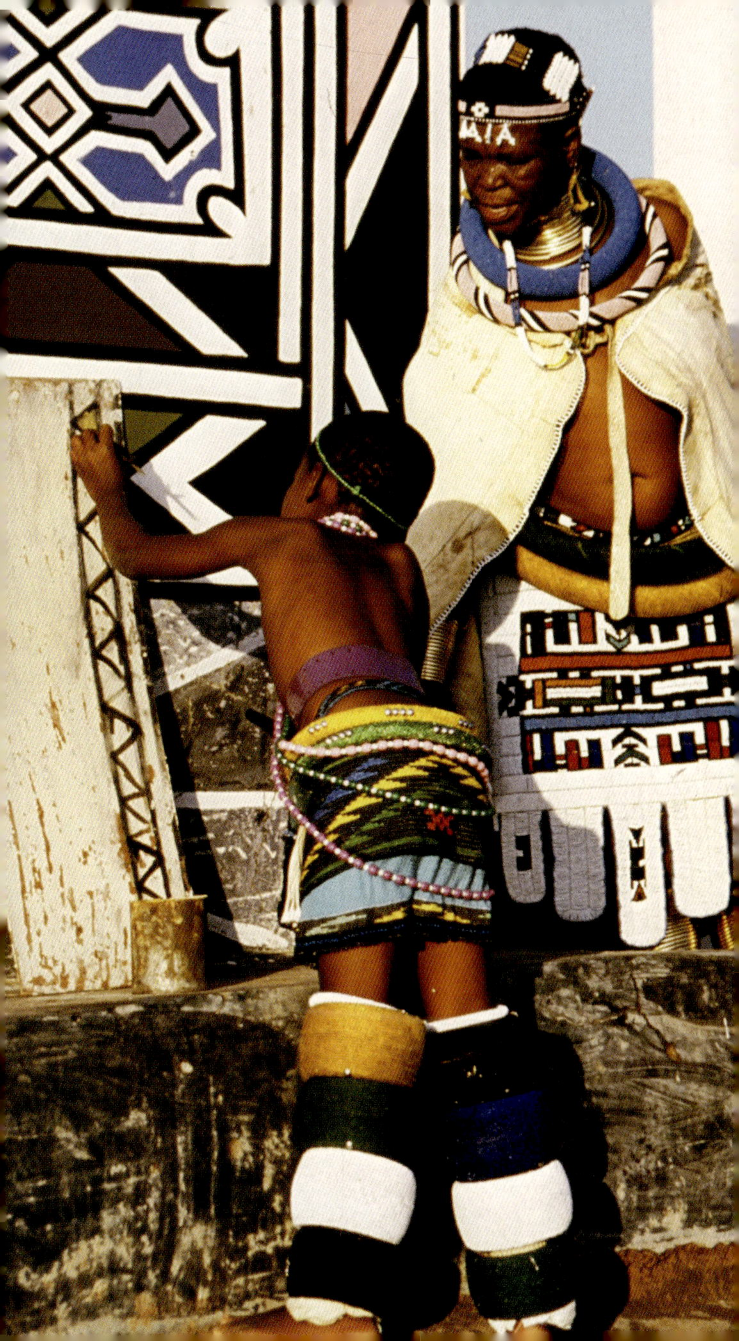

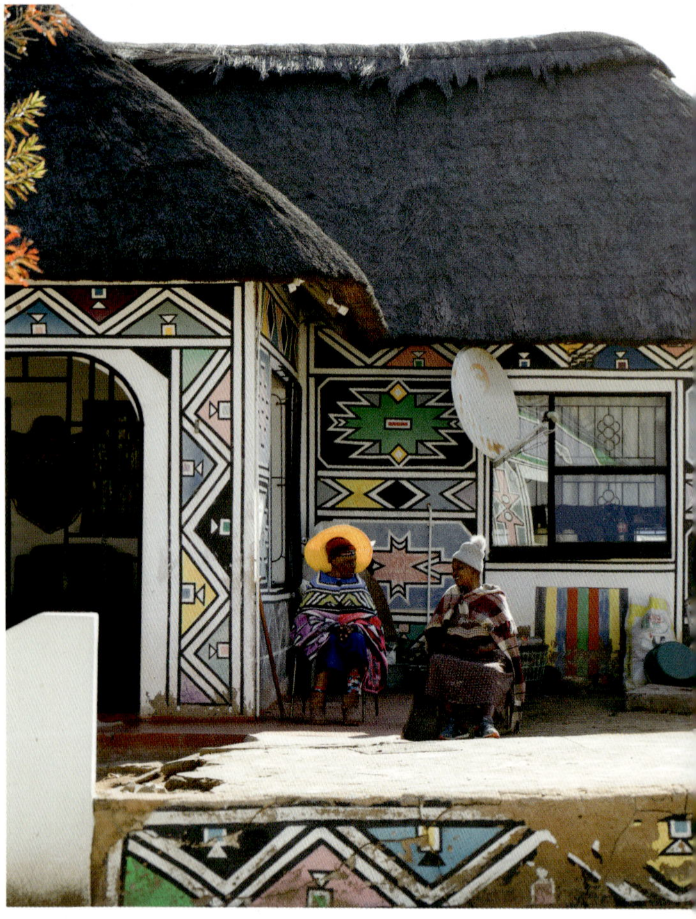

Esther Mahlangu's homestead, Mpumalanga, South Africa, 2023

Mahlangu at work on dashboard art for the Roll
Royce known as "The Mahlangu Phantom," 202

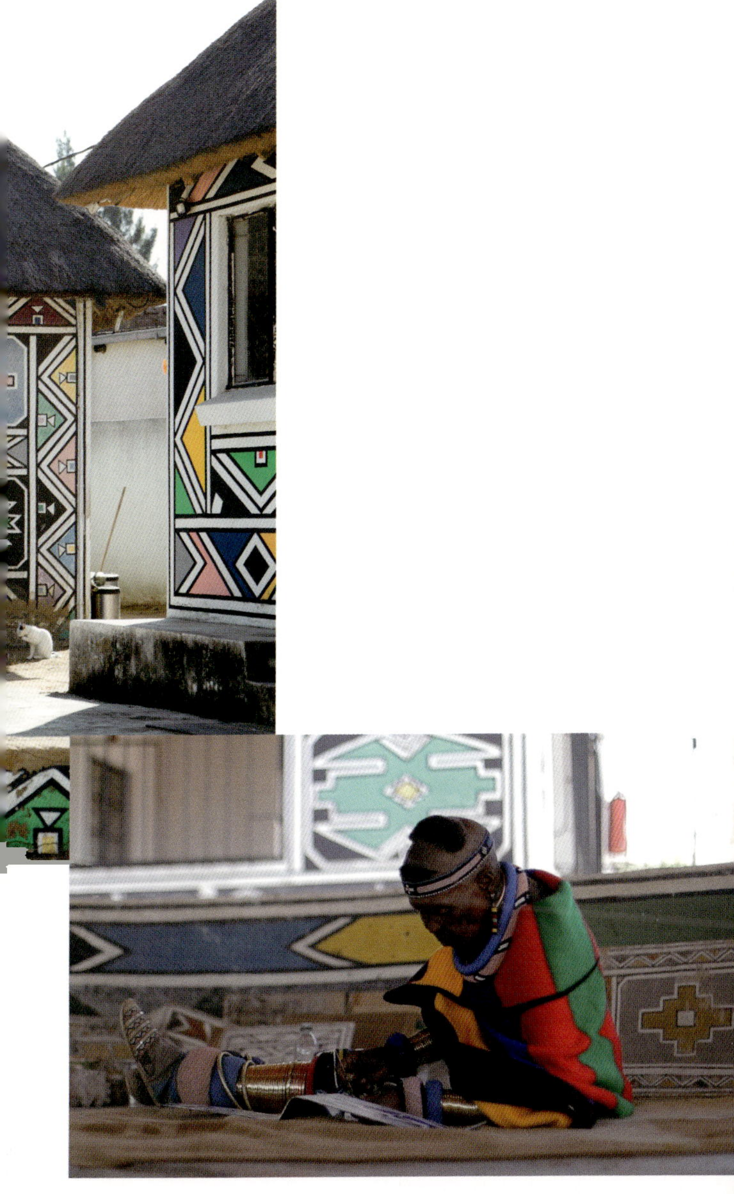

understanding of her heritage. It enabled her to engage with diverse audiences from around the globe, fostering a broader appreciation for her artistic practice and its cultural relevance. As her career expanded beyond the museum, these lessons proved essential to developing her professional career. These experiences also reinforced her belief in the transformative power of art as a tool for storytelling and cultural affirmation and as a catalyst for discourse that challenged and redefined conventional narratives about Indigenous creative practices. This period also marked a turning point in Mahlangu's artistic journey, as she began to see the potential of her work to transcend boundaries and connect with broader audiences beyond her immediate circle of influence. It established the foundation for her collaboration with international institutions, organizations, and brands, positioning her as an ambassador for Ndebele culture on the world stage.

In the late 1980s, Mahlangu's vibrant wall paintings—distinguished by bold color combinations and innovative reinterpretations of Ndebele motifs—caught the attention of international curators, including André Magnin, a commissioner of the landmark exhibition *Magiciens de la Terre* (Magicians of the Earth). In 1989, she was invited to Paris to participate in the exhibition, curated by Jean-Hubert Martin, then director of the Musée National d'Art Moderne at the Centre Pompidou. Mahlangu painstakingly painted a slightly smaller reproduction of her home and its surrounding walls during the show's run. She appeared in the museum in full traditional dress, including the intricately beaded clothing essential to Ndebele customs and aesthetics. Participating in *Magiciens de la Terre* was the launching pad that led to the exponential growth in Mahlangu's acclaim as a visual artist, with projects ranging from a 1991 BMW Art Car to a 2014 artist residency at the Virginia Museum of Fine Arts.

This exposure on the international stage was not only a personal triumph for Mahlangu but a pivotal moment for recognizing Ndebele art within the global art community. Fresh and contemporary in its impact, her work challenged the Western art establishment's preconceived notions about Indigenous and African art forms and art-making strategies. Despite thirty-five years of international prominence, Mahlangu—now almost ninety—continues to live in her village in Mpumalanga province, maintaining her lifelong connection to the traditional Ndebele culture and community. She keeps a studio there and continues to make art, a testament to her enduring commitment to expanding her artistic practice, pursuing her creative curiosity, and carrying forward the inspiration of her heritage. Through her art, Esther Mahlangu not only preserves the traditions of her ancestors but also ensures that they continue to inspire and resonate in new ways across generations and continents.

Endnote
1. Heléne Smuts and Chonat Getz, "Knowledge in Translation," *Esther Mahlangu 80* (Cape Town: UCT Irma Stern Museum, 2015), 18.

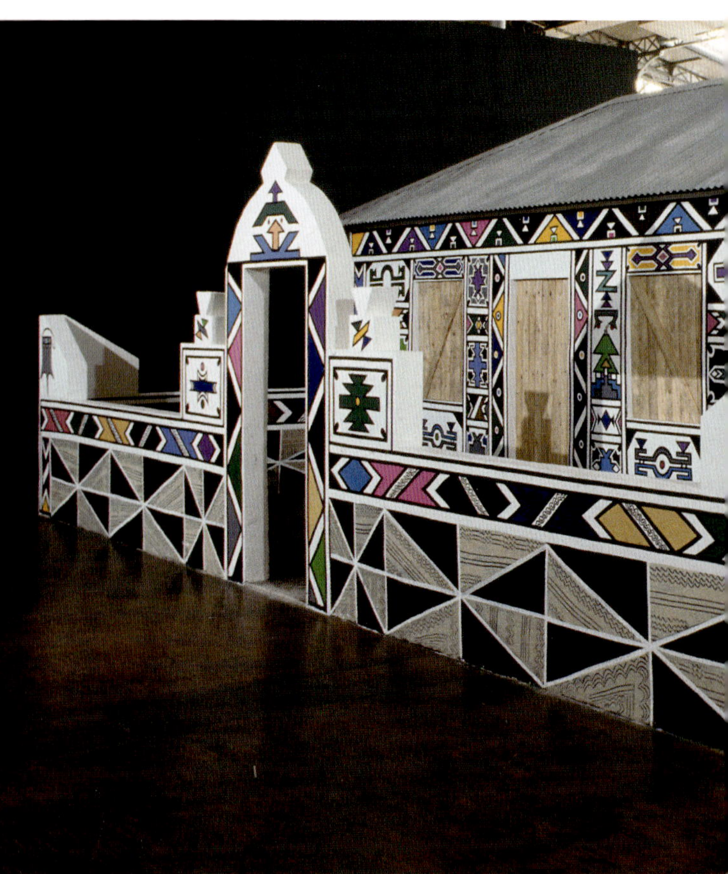

At the Centre Pompidou in Paris, Mahlangu painted a slightly small-scale reproduction of her home for the 1989 exhibition *Magiciens de la Terre*. It was her first participation in a major international exhibition. The experience led Mahlangu to a new understanding of how Ndebele culture and her own art could be represented in the world.

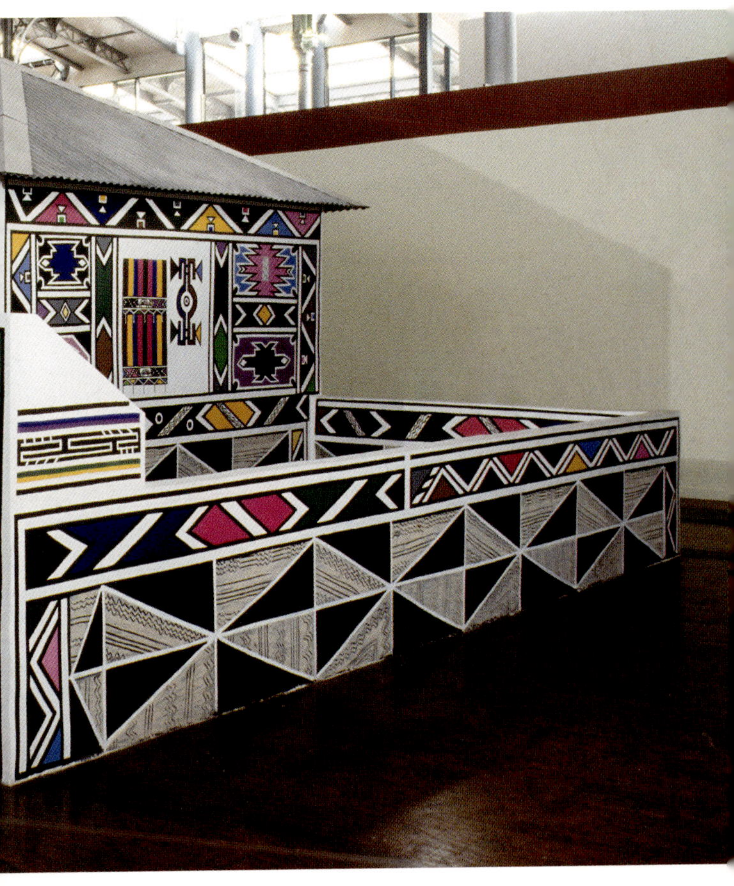

Installation view of Mahlangu's artwork in *Magiciens de la Terre*
(Magicians of the Earth), Centre Pompidou, 1989

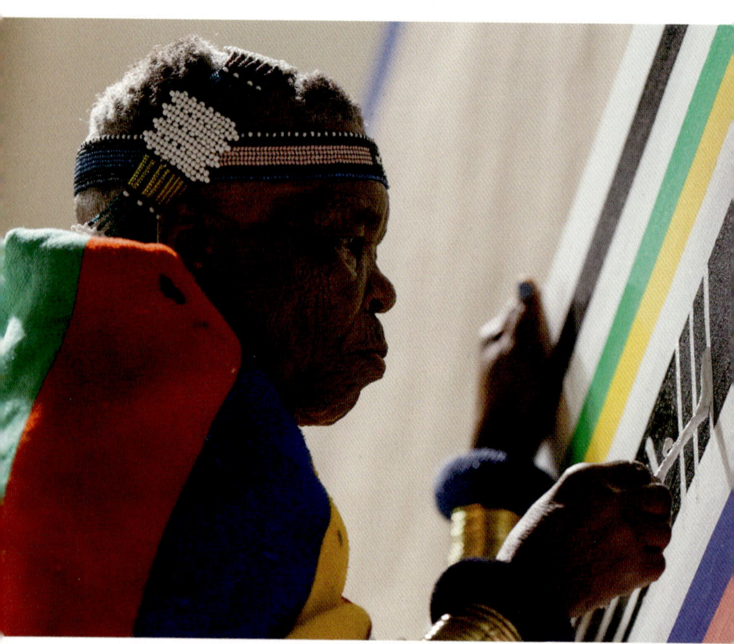

Mahlangu at work on a wall-mural canvas for the Virginia Museum of Fine Arts, 2014

MAHLANGU'S ART: A CLOSER LOOK

In Ndebele culture, geometric patterns are profound symbols of community and cosmic order. Geometric abstraction is a critical element of Mahlangu's practice, with rectangles, triangles, chevrons, and diamonds used to create compositions emphasizing form, line, composition and color over representation. In Ndebele tradition, these patterns have signaled essential life events such as weddings, resulting in a visual language communicated across generations. Mahlangu's imaginative approach breathes new life into these traditional forms as she pushes the boundaries of geometric abstraction. Her inventive use of color and unique rhythm and balance allows her to express complex ideas and emotions that resonate with and beyond her cultural heritage, even as she pays homage to her ancestors. Unity, rhythm, symmetry, and balance—hallmarks of geometric abstraction and Ndebele art—are integral to Mahlangu's work. Through her creativity, she re-envisions these ancient symbols in a contemporary context, celebrating Ndebele culture and the evolving expression of her artistic vision.

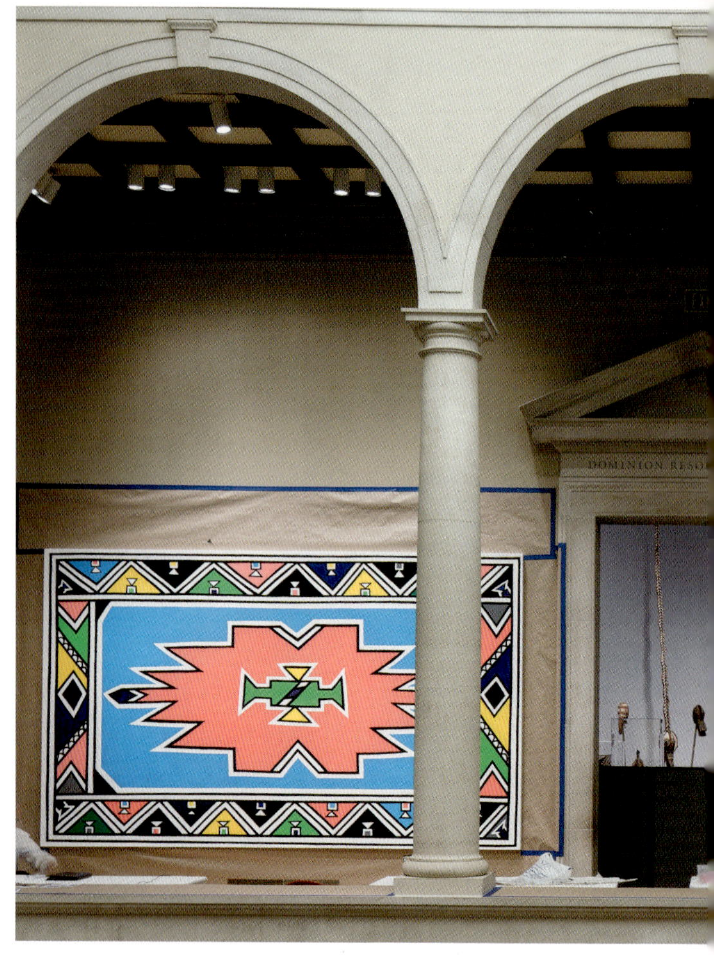

Imabala

One prominent motif in Mahlangu's work is *Imabala*, a tribute to the matriarchs in her family who shaped her artistic journey. Distinctive to Mahlangu's practice, *Imabala* reflects her creative reinterpretation of traditional Ndebele patterns. When painting this motif,

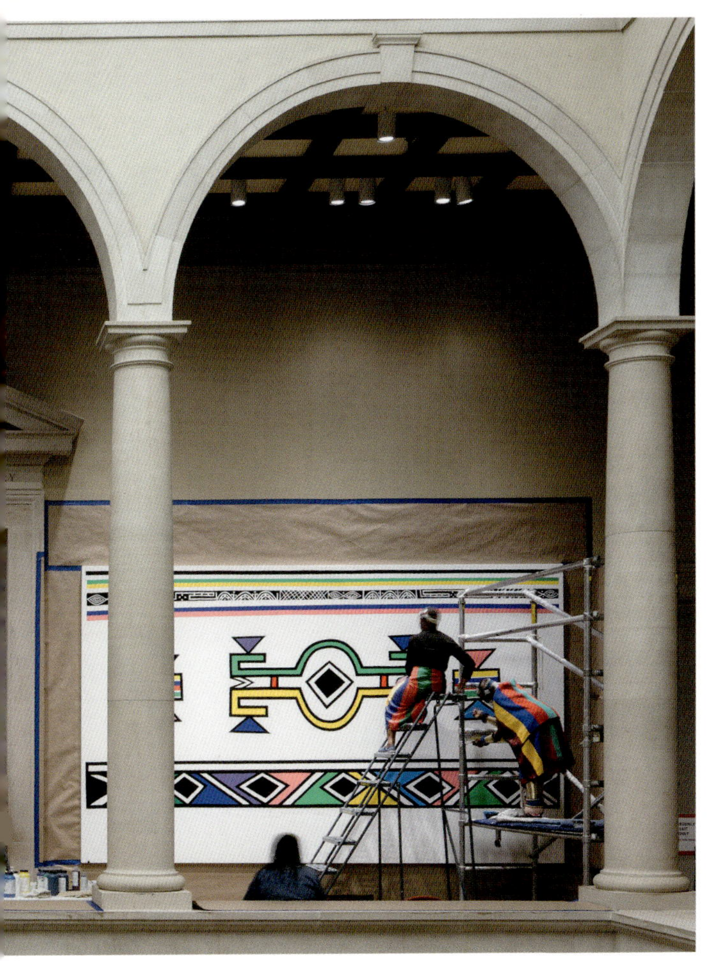

particularly in murals, Mahlangu insists on executing it herself, underscoring its significance. This intimate approach imbues her work with layers of meaning, creating a bridge between the past and present.

At the Virginia Museum of Fine Arts, Mahlangu (assisted by her granddaughter Marriam) paints the central *Imabala* motif on one of the two wall-sized canvases she created for the museum in 2014.

The *Imabala* motif anchors many of Mahlangu's compositions. The contrasting gold and blue of the *Imabala* in this work sets off the diamond shape at its center.

Mahlangu has said that she is looking to create a sense of balance, peace, and harmony in her art, achieved through the placement of shapes and colors across the composition.

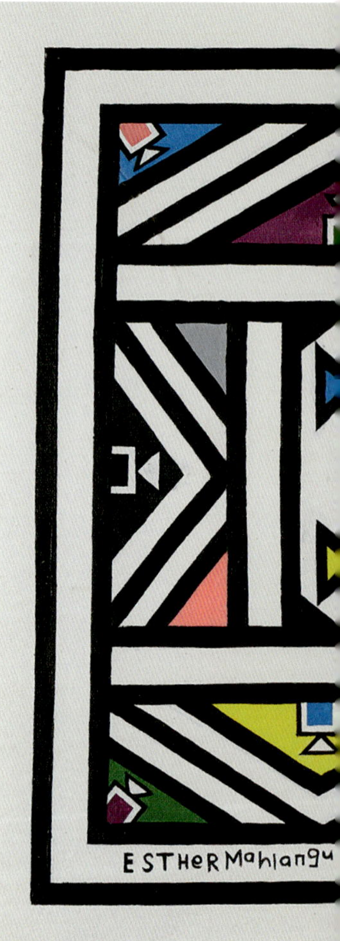

Untitled (Ndebele Abstract), 2011
Acrylic paint on canvas
27 x 35 inches (70 x 90 cm)

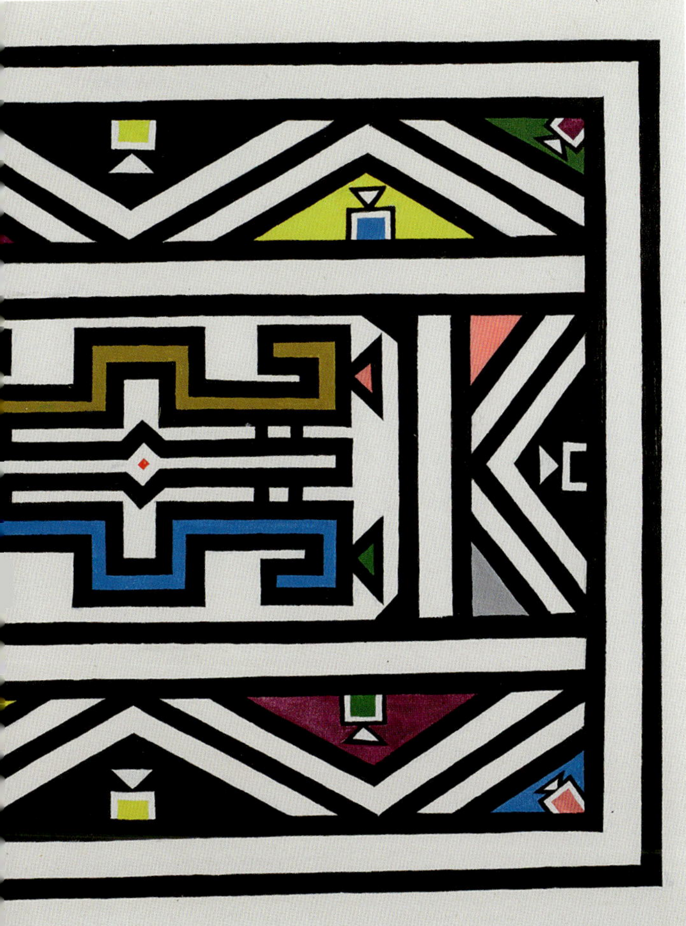

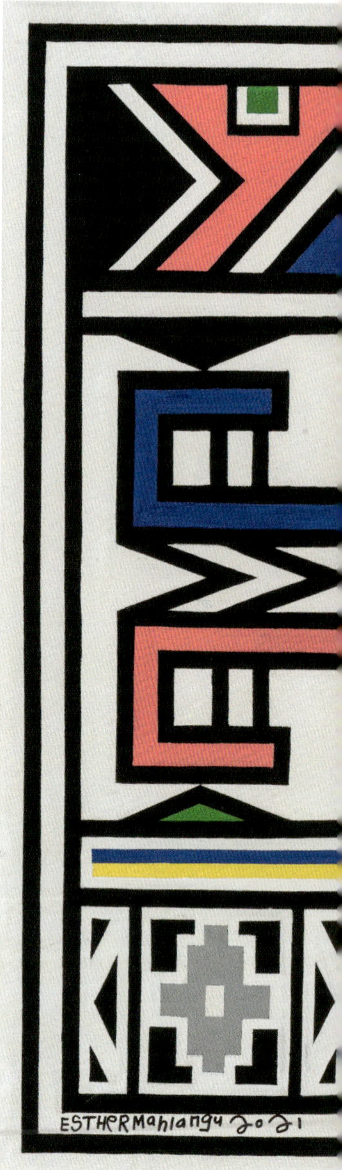

Mahlangu often pairs the *Imabala* motif with a contrasting visual element—in this case, the black, white, and gray shapes that are the painting's foundational layer.

Ndebele Abstract, 2021
Acrylic paint on canvas
47 ¼ x 47 ¼ inches (120 x 120 cm)

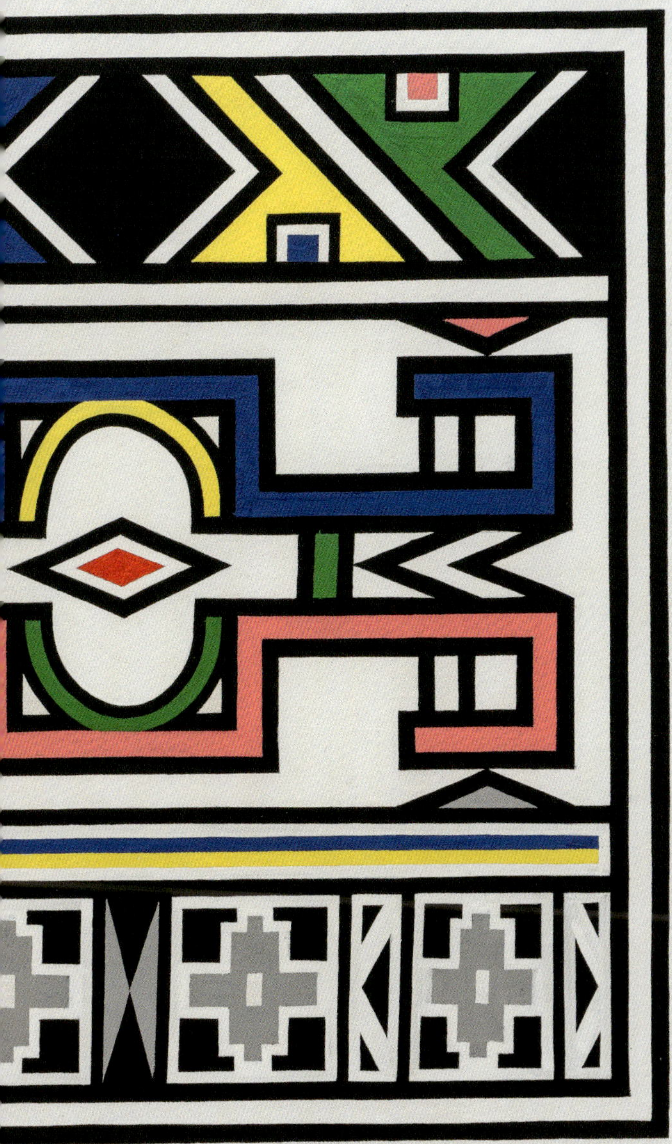

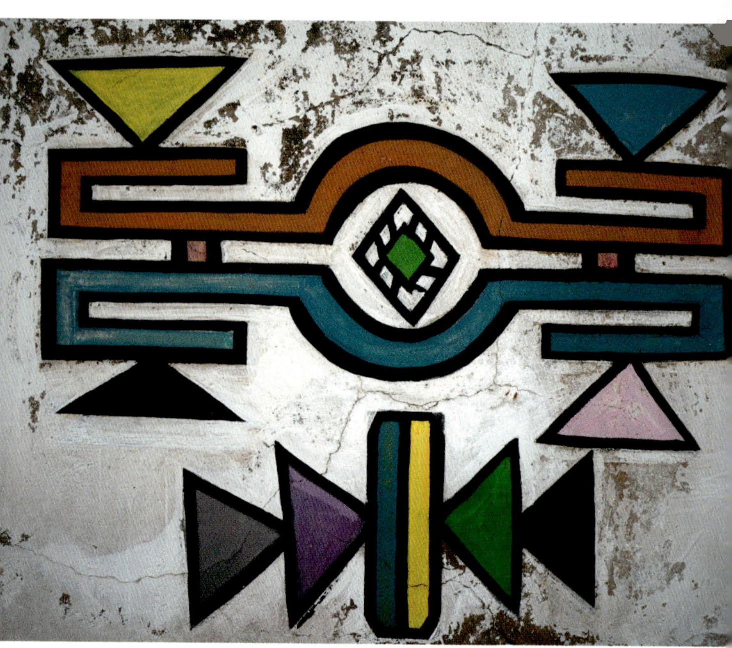

Mahlangu painted these two *Imabala* motifs on her home. While her canvas works often feature *Imabala* motifs rendered horizontally, she occasionally employs vertical versions in architectural settings.

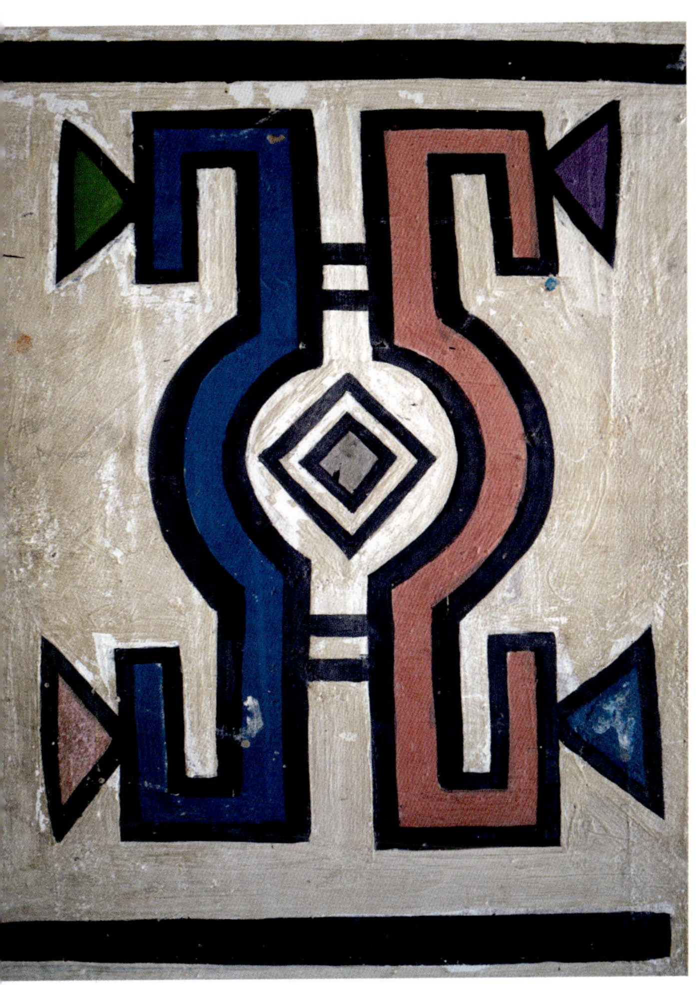

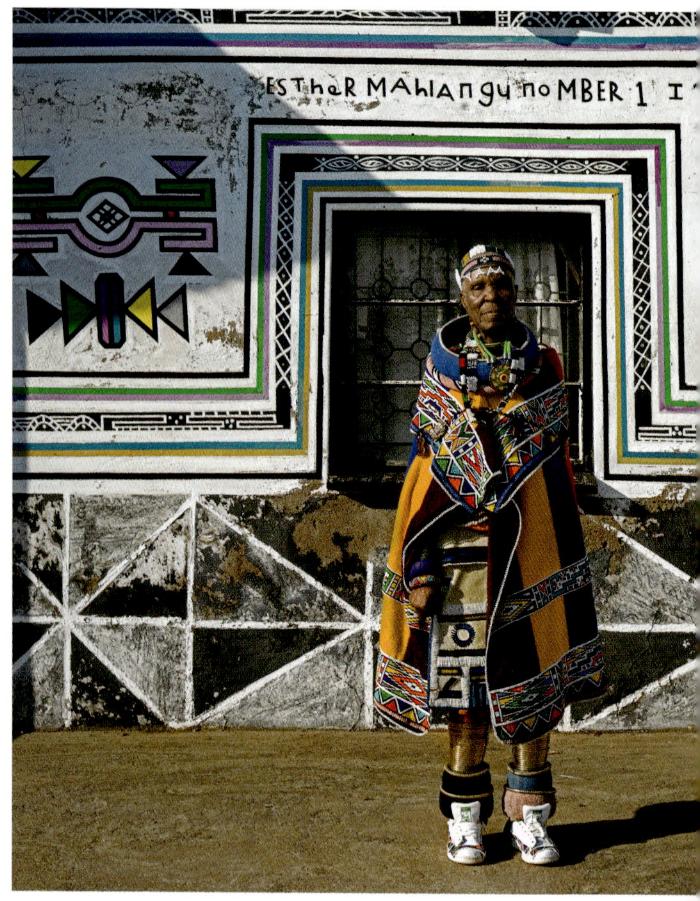

Esther Mahlangu in front of one of the buildings at her
homestead, Mpumalanga, South Africa, 2020

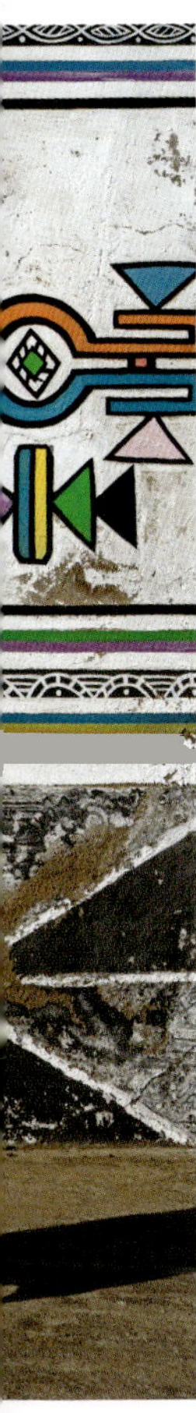

Here, Mahlangu stands before a wall of her home, painted in her vibrant designs. She's framed by horizontal *Imabala* motifs, including the one on page 32. *Imabala* is one of several recurring motifs Mahlangu incorporates into her murals. At ground level is a large black, white, and gray pattern known as *Ikughuphu*—another key element in her visual language.

Ikughuphu

Ikughuphu forms a foundational layer in Mahlangu's work. Often rendered in gray, black, and white tones, it appears across her murals, wall paintings, and large-scale canvases. Painted with her fingers or delicate feather brushes, *Ikughuphu* is infused with ancestral patterns and spiritual resonance—an homage to Ndebele heritage and Mahlangu's connection to those who came before her.

When creating this layer, Mahlangu often manipulates the wet paint with her fingers, adding stripes, waves, or subtle texture. We see this technique on the following page: the design has already begun to take shape in the painting on the wall behind her. And in a striking twist, she's mid-process, adding that same detail to an unexpected surface—the body of Somali-born supermodel Iman.

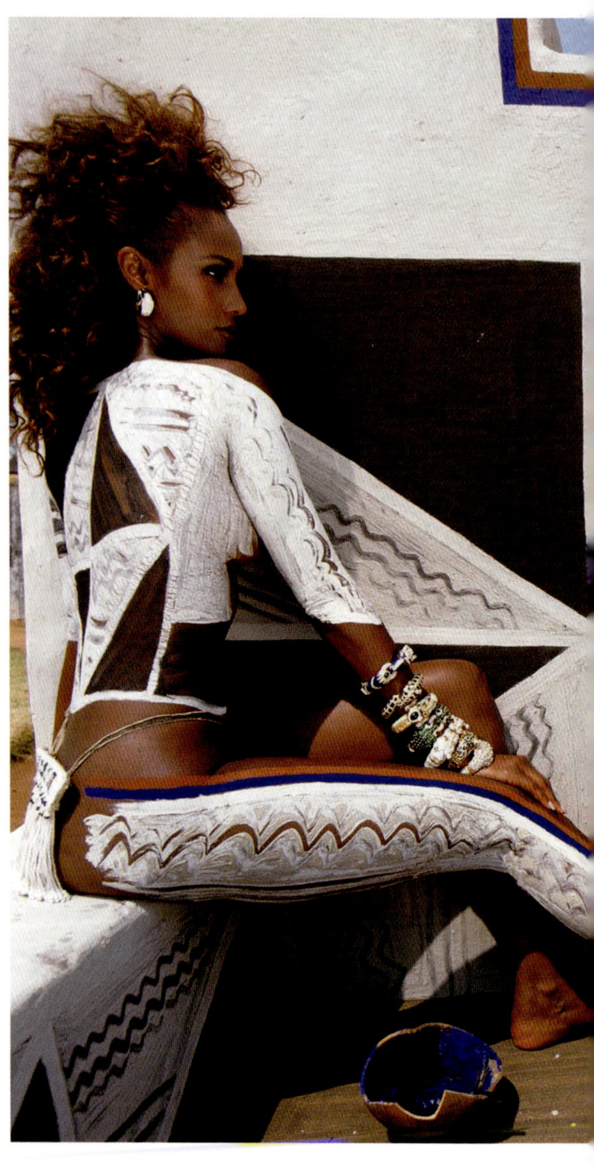

Esther Mahlangu painting the supermodel Iman in South Africa,1991

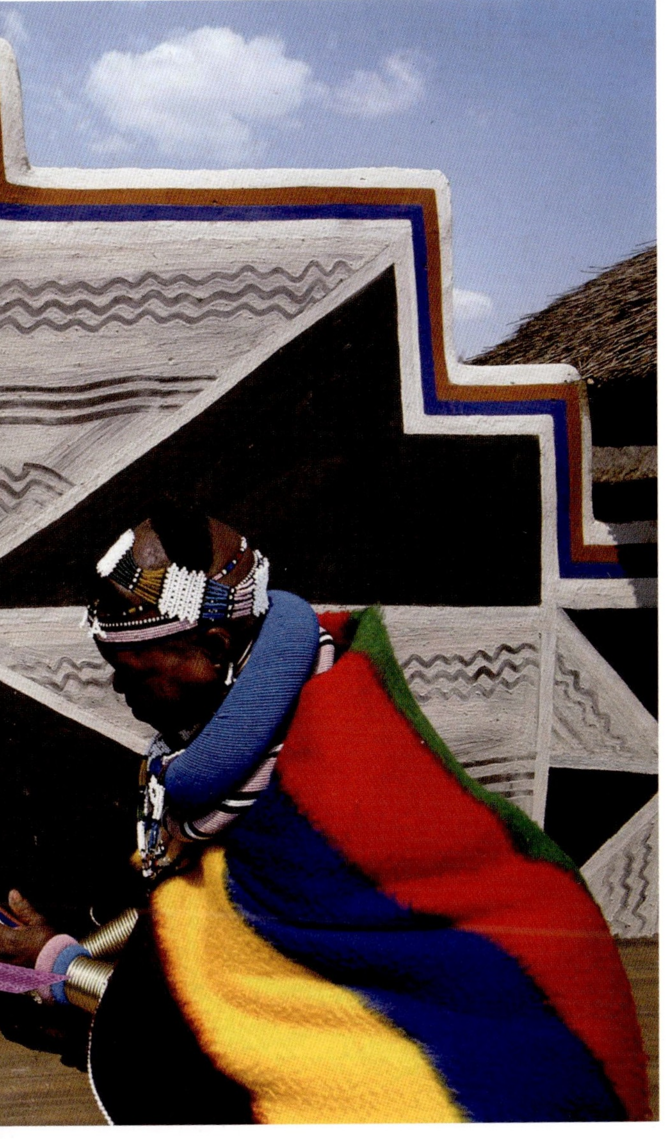

Mahlangu paints the *Ikughuphu* layer of a 9 × 15-foot mural—one of two she created during a 2014 residency at the Virginia Museum of Fine Arts in Richmond, Virginia. She incorporates the foundational composition that grounds the rest of the work with swift, intuitive movements, layering ancestral memory into this monumental artwork.

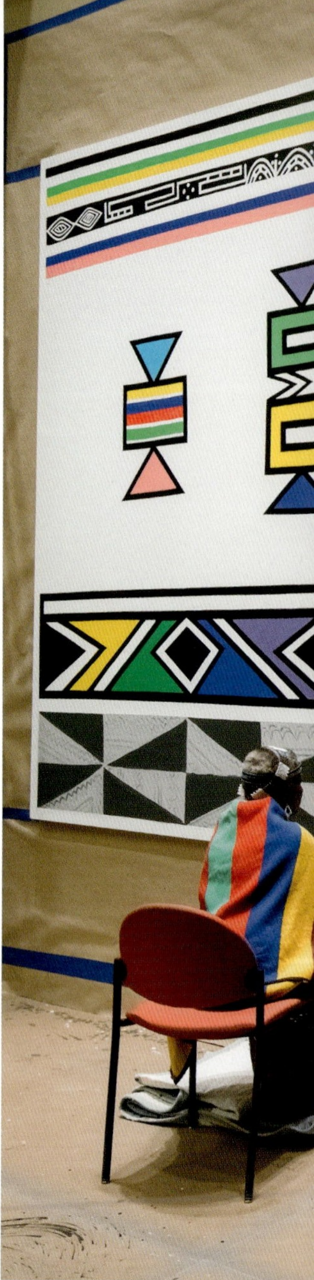

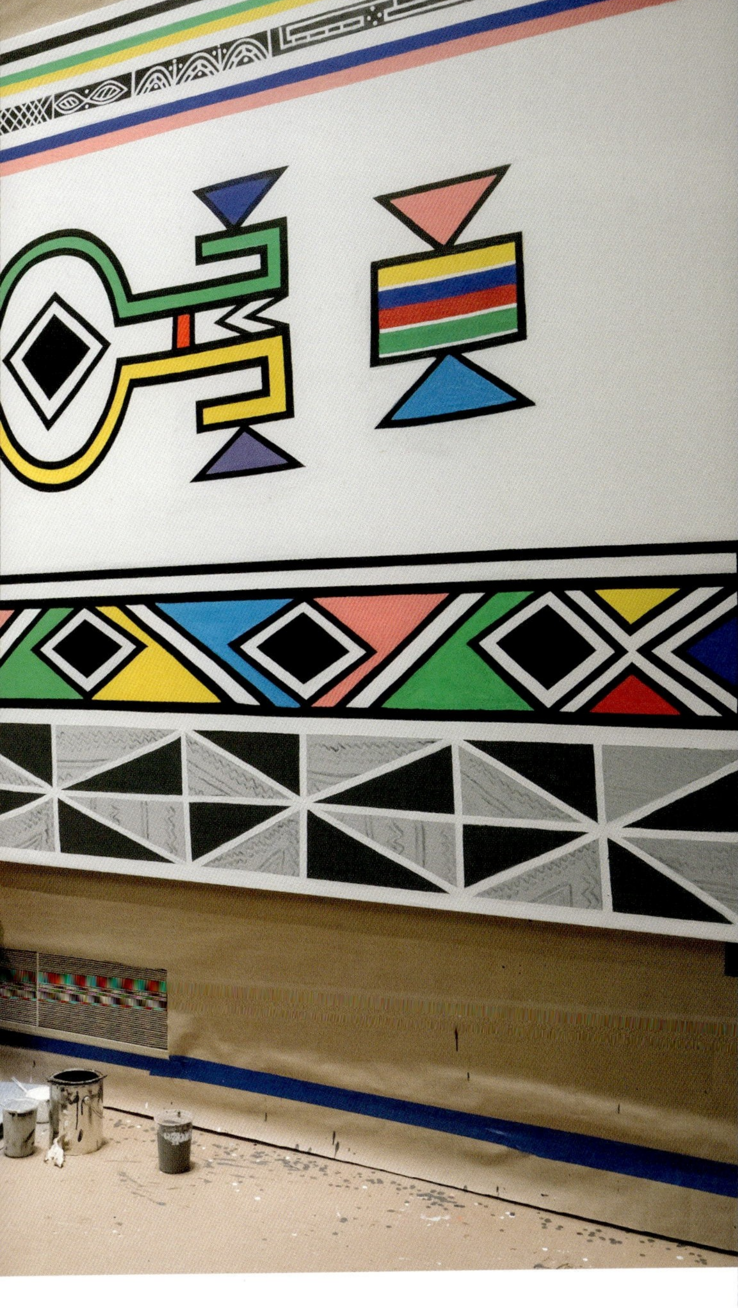

Razor blade / Tshefana

Perhaps most strikingly, Mahlangu's use of the razor blade, or *tshefana*, stands out as her signature motif. Specifically, she features the Minora blade, a staple of South African life with cultural and utilitarian significance since the 1950s. In Ndebele rituals, the blade serves as a tool for beadwork and other crafts, while in daily life it's used for shaving and hairstyling. Mahlangu's abstracted razor motifs transform this ordinary object into a catalyst for reflection, offering viewers multiple entry points to engage with her ideas. Similarly, her large-scale works—murals, installations, and wall-sized paintings—redefine everyday spaces by incorporating quotidian elements.

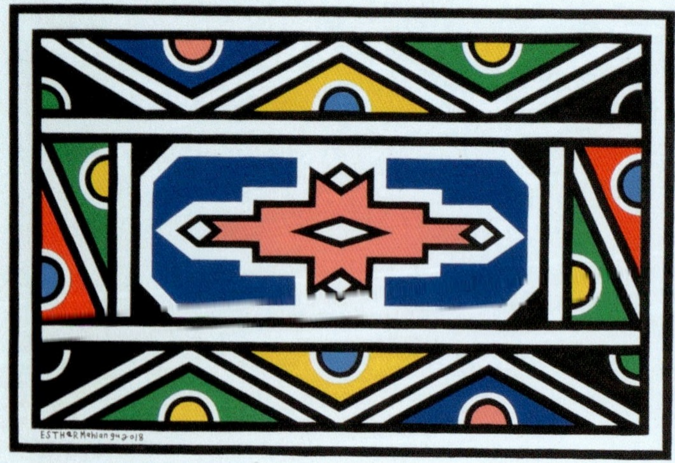

Untitled (Ndebele Abstract), 2011
Acrylic paint on canvas
47 x 67 inches (120 x 170 cm)

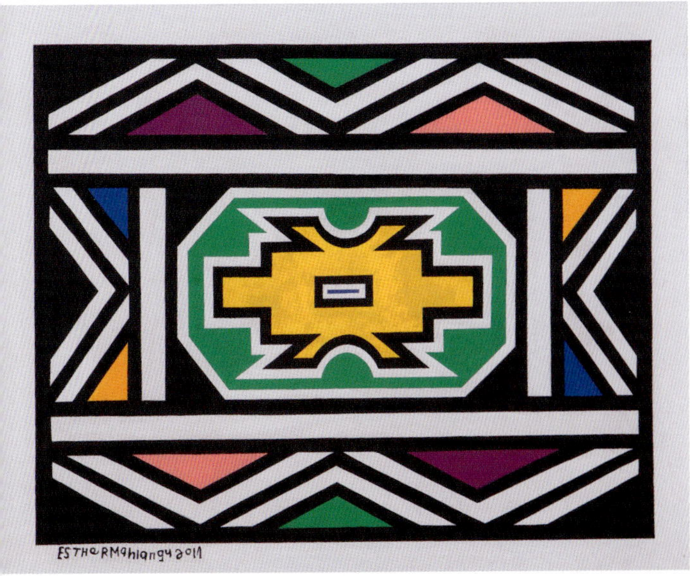

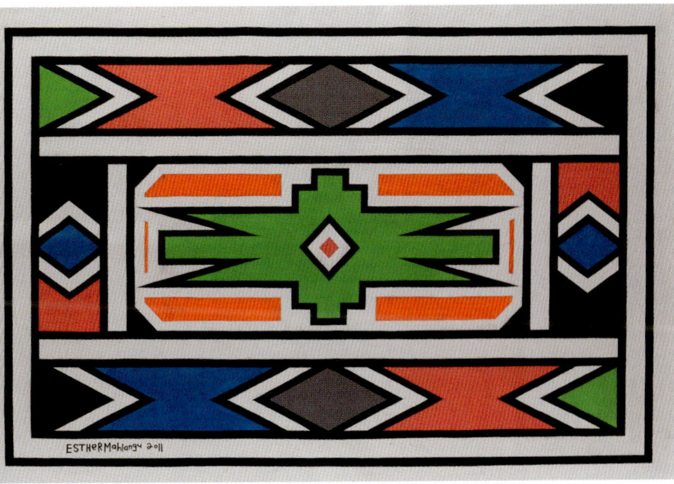

above
***Untitled (Ndebele Abstract)**, 2011*
Acrylic paint on canvas
39 3/8 x 59 inches (100 x 150 cm)

below
***Untitled (Ndebele Abstract)**, 2011*
Acrylic paint on canvas
43 x 67 inches (110 x 170 cm)

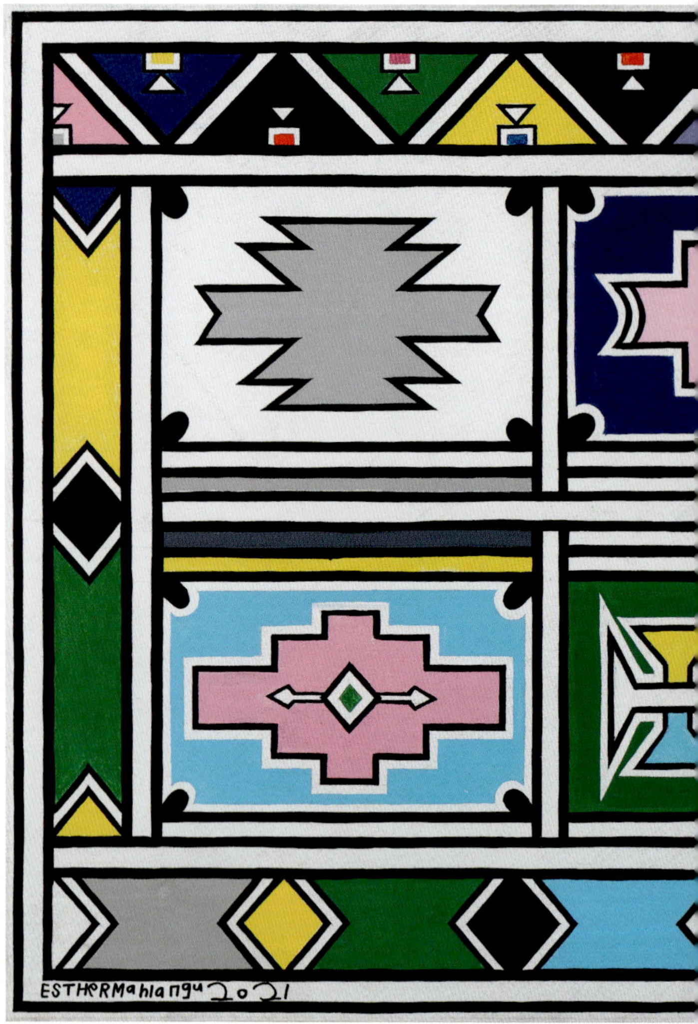

Untitled (Ndebele Abstract), 2021
Acrylic paint on canvas
39 3/8 x 59 inches (100 x 150 cm)

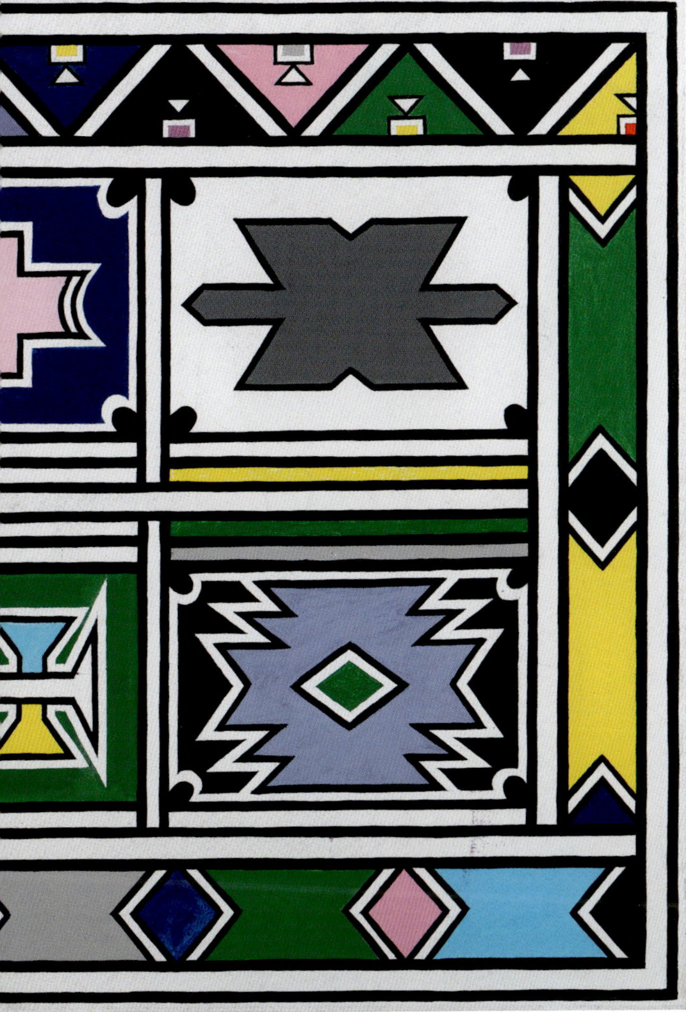

Streets Lamps and Houses

Mahlangu incorporates an ensemble of imagery from the everyday, such as street lamps, light bulbs, and houses, which metaphorically serve as ancestral portals. In some works, these symbols reference her homestead near a coal mine, subtly timestamping her environment while hinting at the lives of those whose labor fueled the town's industry. Mahlangu's use of industrial hard hats as a surface for her art (see page 55) gestures toward this history—a quiet acknowledgment of the miners whose work defined the region's identity yet often remained unseen. By embedding these seemingly mundane elements into her compositions, Mahlangu transforms them into markers of memory, cultural continuity, and resilience. As ancestral portals, these motifs also serve as conduits for spiritual connection, linking the living with those who came before, imbuing her work with reverence and rootedness.

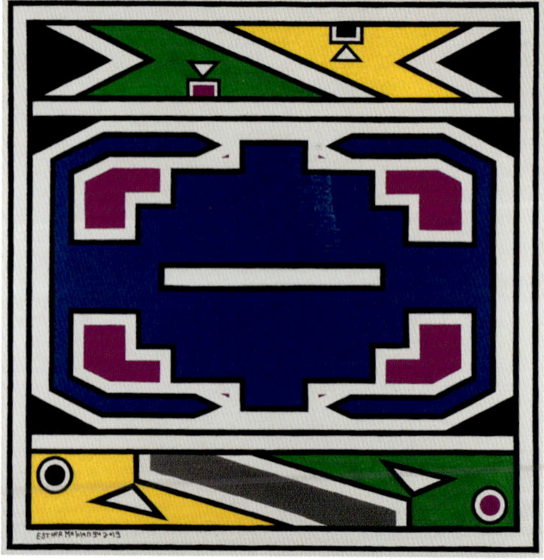

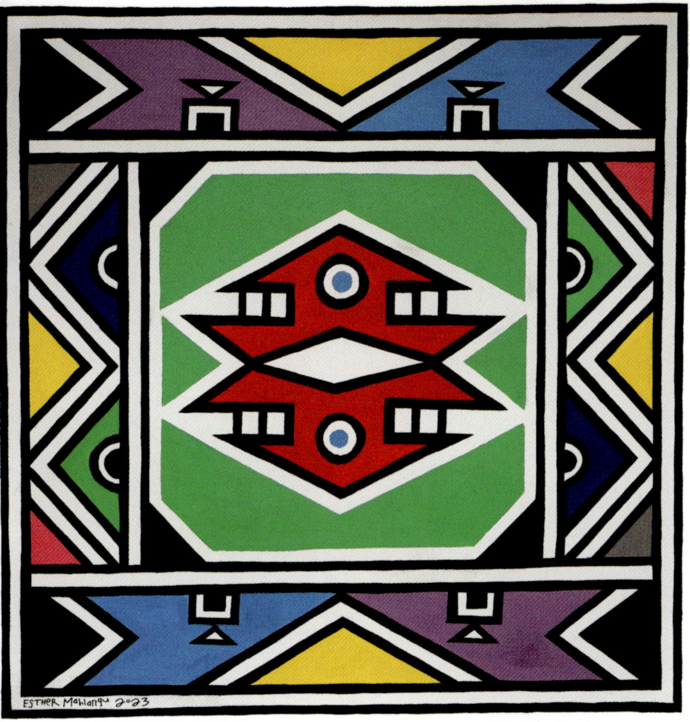

Untitled, 2023; close-up detail

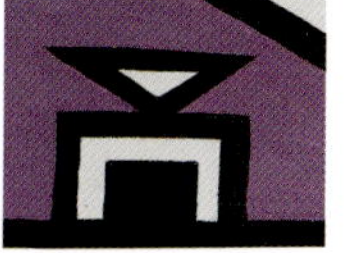

Mahlangu often draws on forms from every-day life, transforming shapes and patterns into evocative, abstracted symbols. In the artwork above, the red motif at the center might suggest a factory, the ridge of a house, a streetlamp, or a beacon. Along the top and bottom edges, small squares topped with triangles—a recurring element in her work—evoke houses, conjuring a sense of village or neighborhood. Similar forms appear in the upper section of the work at the left, linking the two paintings through a shared visual language of home and community.

above
Untitled, 2023; close-up detail
Acrylic paint on canvas
47 ¹/₄ x 47 ¹/₄ inches (120 x 120 cm)

opposite
Untitled, 2020
Acrylic paint on canvas
63 x 63 inches (160 x 160 cm)

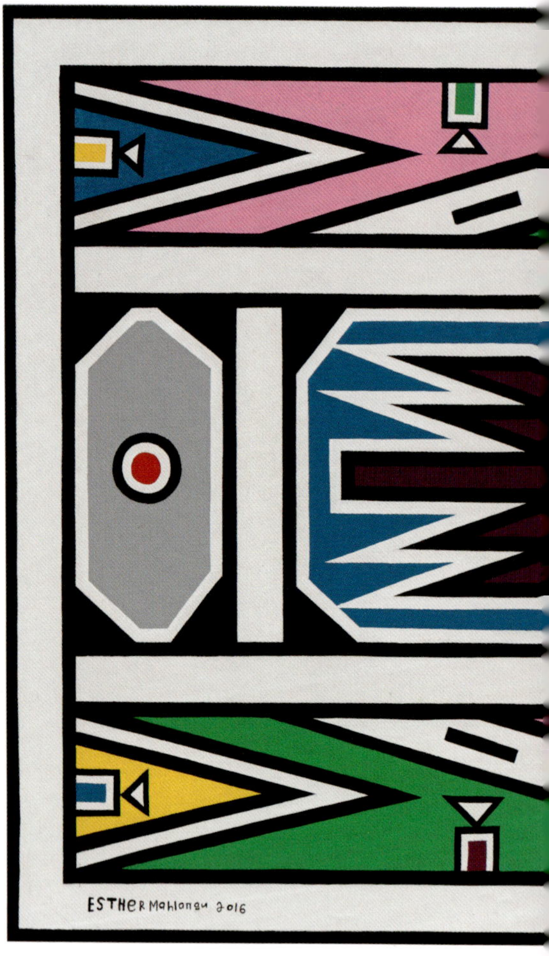

While Mahlangu prefers not to interpret or explain her work, this painting evokes the layout of a village or neighborhood. The geometric shapes in the upper and lower bands are anchored by motifs representing traditional houses. Diagonal white strips with broken lines suggest pathways or roads connecting the community. At the center, Mahlangu has placed an abstract interpretation of her signature motif, the razor blade, highlighting its cultural significance within the composition's spatial narrative.

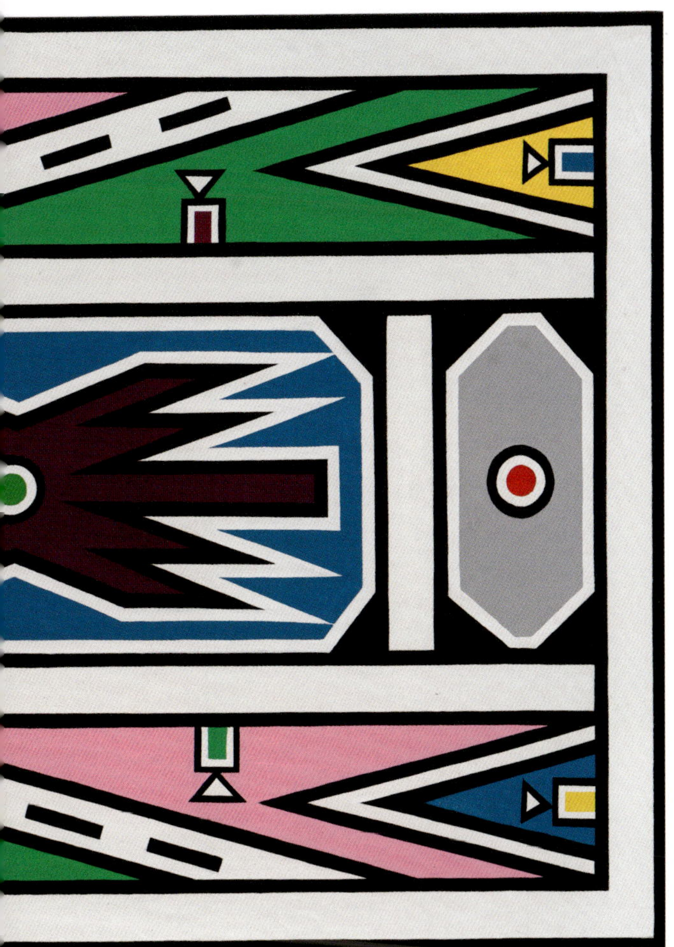

Untitled (Ndebele Abstract), 2016
Acrylic paint on canvas
47 x 47 inches (119.4 x 119.4 cm)

Hand-Painted Geometries

From a distance, Mahlangu's paintings are striking in their hard-edged accuracy. Reflecting the traditions of Ndebele art, every line and shape is painted freehand, without the use of stencils, rulers, masking tape, or other aids.

A closer look brings that handmade quality into vivid focus. What from a distance look like straight, hard edges are, in close-up, a bit softer. Each line and shape is clearly composed of individual brush strokes, with tiny variations in the application of the paint. Together, these minute imperfections—invisible unless you're really looking for them—give Mahlangu's art a human presence and energy beyond their geometry and pattern.

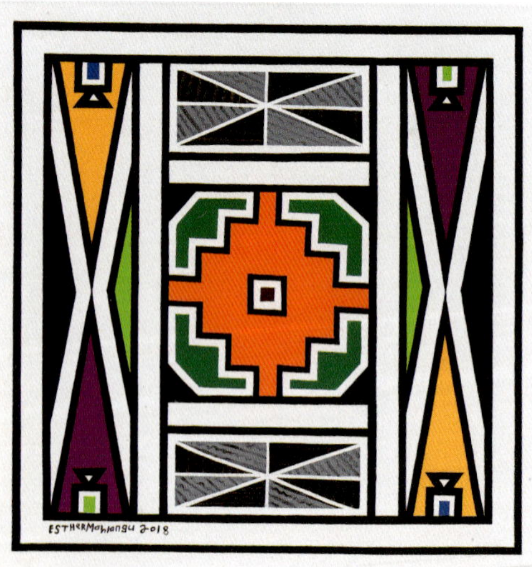

***Untitled (Ndebele Abstract)**, 2018; opposite: close-up detail*
Acrylic paint on canvas
47 x 47 inches (119.4 x 119.4 cm)

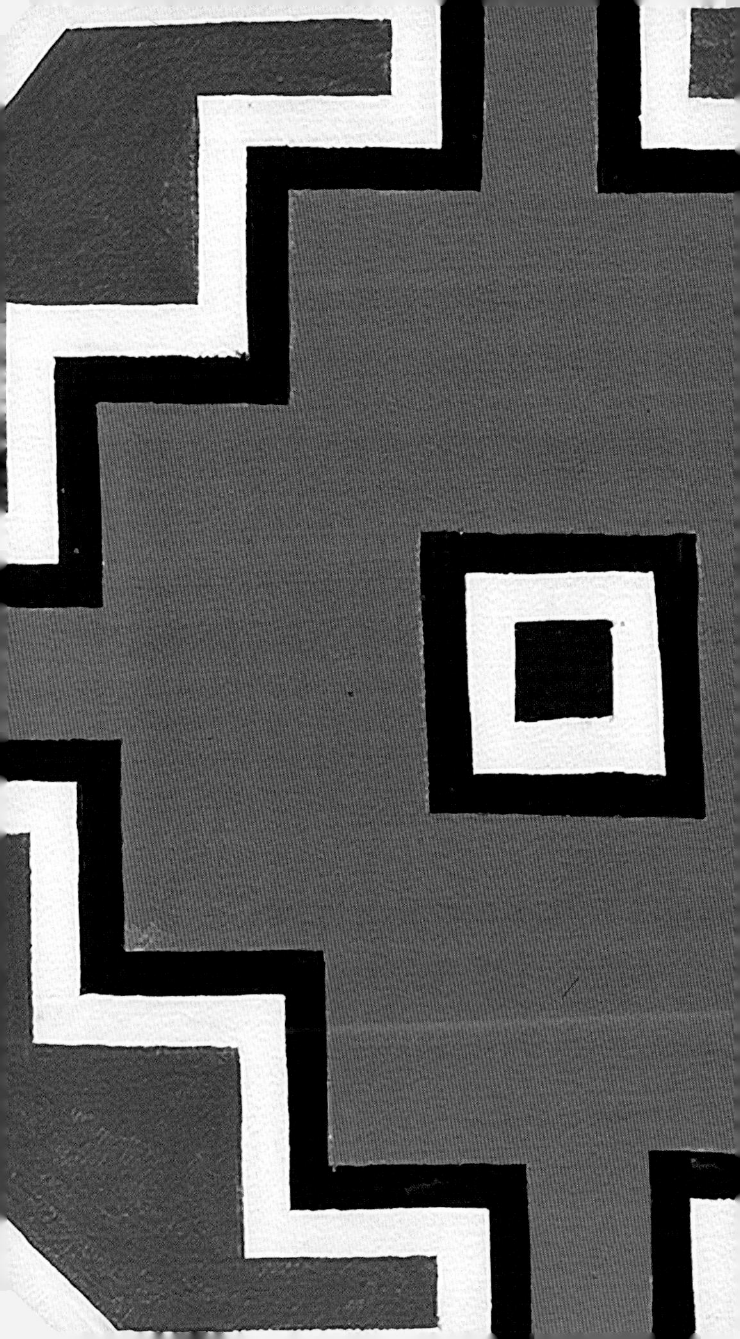

Pigment and Paint

During her childhood, Mahlangu learned traditional methods of creating pigments by mixing naturally colored soil with cow dung and water, producing the earthy tones used by Ndebele artists for generations. As time passed, Mahlangu and other Ndebele women gained access to industrial-grade house paints, offering a broader palette of colors. This expanded range of color options enriched Mahlangu's work and opened new creative pathways for her and her Ndebele contemporaries.

Mahlangu's artistic practice evolved significantly as her work garnered international attention. Her adoption of acrylic paints marked a pivotal moment in her journey, as these materials offered a broader spectrum of colors than traditional pigments and house paints. Moreover, it enabled Mahlangu to go beyond tradition and cultivate her aesthetic. This expanded palette allowed Mahlangu to experiment with bold, unconventional color combinations, redefining the visual language of her practice. "Acrylic paints have allowed me to use many more colors than I could have with natural pigments," Mahlangu has said, underscoring how this change has brought her compositions to life in new ways. Today, acrylics are Mahlangu's preferred medium, embodying her relentless drive to innovate and push the boundaries of her art.

"**Acrylic** paints have allowed me to use many more colors than I could have with natural pigments," Mahlangu has said. Her love of unconventional color combinations is evident in these exuberant mannequin torsos. Mahlangu includes a deep layer of *Ikughuphu* in black, white, and gray on each mannequin's legs and pelvis—a move that grounds even these fanciful works in traditional Ndebele art.

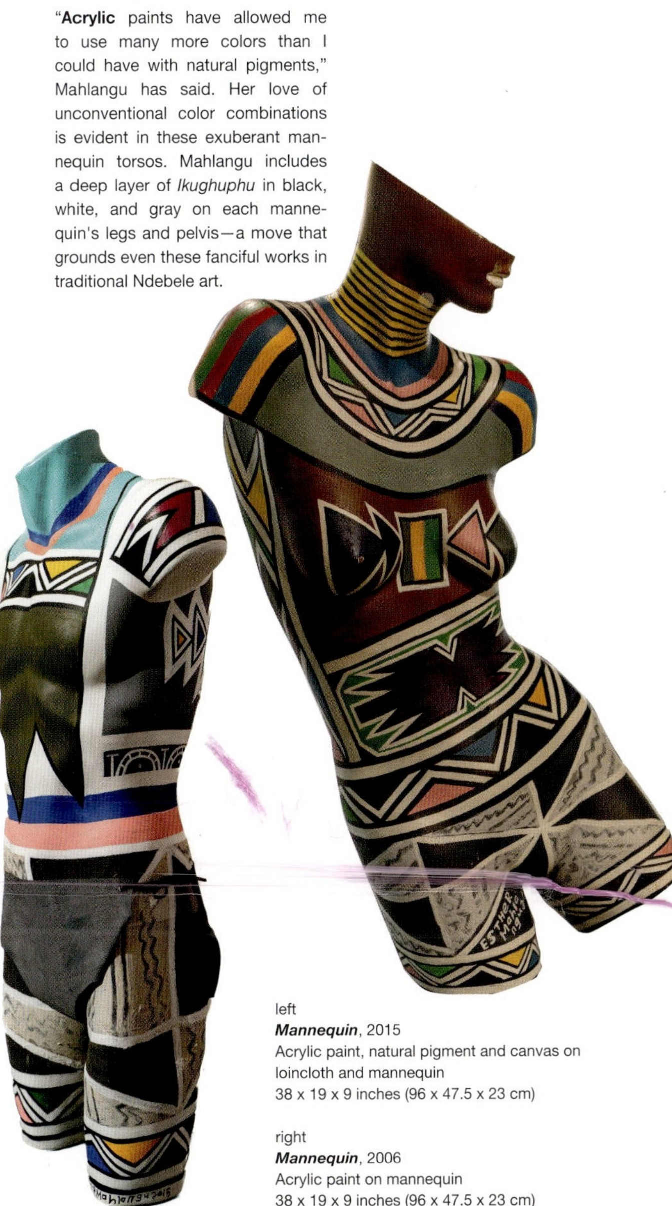

left
Mannequin, 2015
Acrylic paint, natural pigment and canvas on loincloth and mannequin
38 x 19 x 9 inches (96 x 47.5 x 23 cm)

right
Mannequin, 2006
Acrylic paint on mannequin
38 x 19 x 9 inches (96 x 47.5 x 23 cm)

By blending traditional Ndebele techniques with contemporary materials, Mahlangu creates a robust dialogue between heritage and innovation. Rooted in her cultural identity but uniquely her own, her work resonates with global audiences and reimagines how we engage with artistic expression. Through her art, Mahlangu redefines tradition, ensuring its vitality and relevance in an ever-evolving world.

Mahlangu's work seamlessly merges traditional practices with contemporary contexts and materials, all filtered through her rich artistic imagination. This creative fusion has enabled her to collaborate with art galleries, cultural institutions, and other entities worldwide, further expanding her influence and the reach of her cultural heritage. "What many find interesting about my artworks," she has said, "is that although they are based on traditional Ndebele designs, they are still very modern and current."[2]

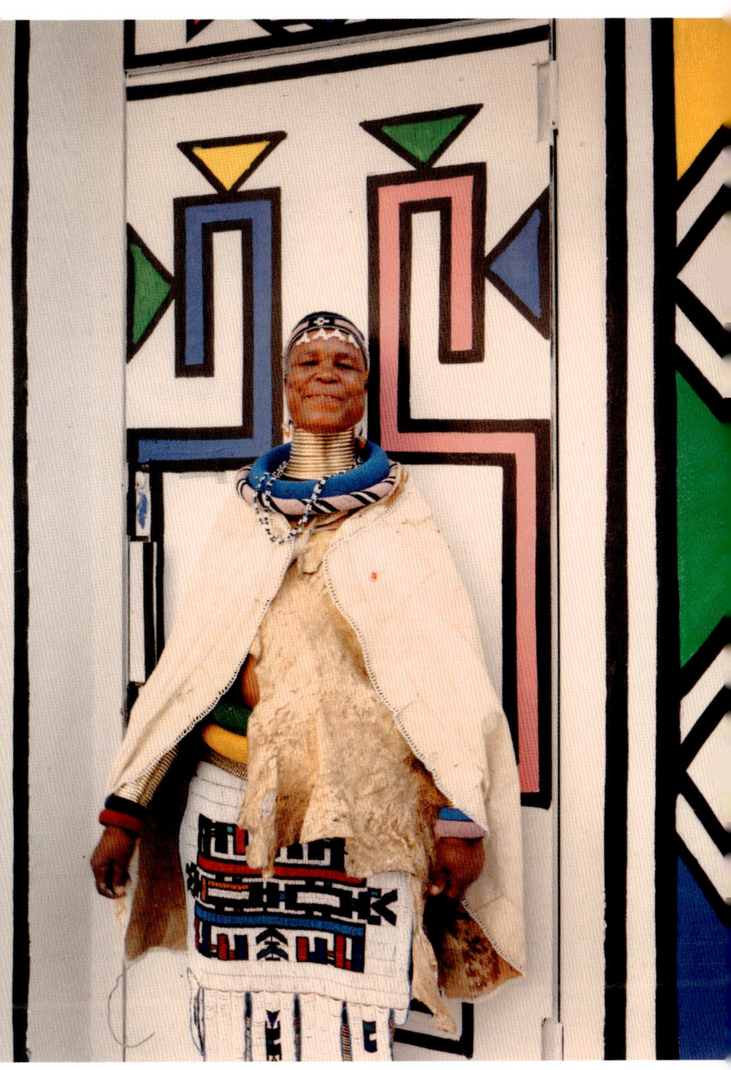

Esther Mahlangu with her façade installation at the National Museum of Women in the Arts, Washington, DC, during the exhibition *Esther Mahlangu, South African Muralist: The BMW Art Car and Related Works*, 1994. She stands before an *Imabala* motif. Here, its vertical orientation emphasizes height and rhythm, aligning the motif with the structure's form and signaling its symbolic significance in lived spaces.

Surface Mastery

Mahlangu's dexterity in working across many surfaces is a superpower. Unlike many contemporary artists whose work becomes synonymous with a specific material, Mahlangu moves seamlessly between "high" and "low" surfaces, her artistry transcending the limitations of traditional or expected materials. Whether painting a BMW, the walls of a museum, or the rounded curves of a Belvedere vodka bottle, Mahlangu navigates each project with an assuredness that testifies to her deep, intuitive understanding of form, space, and texture. The ability to adapt her art to these various surfaces without diluting its essence demonstrates skill and a profound cultural intelligence—a commitment to honoring her heritage while developing an extensive artistic oeuvre.

What sets Mahlangu apart is her willingness to engage unconventional surfaces and her capacity to assert control over any material presented to her. A hard hat's curved shell offers as much possibility as a gallery wall. This adaptability is not about compromise but about expansiveness; it is a declaration that her art and hands are not restricted to the domestic, the rural, or the ethnographic. By moving fluidly between "fine art" and the utilitarian—painting museum walls as quickly as hard hats or skate decks—Mahlangu dissolves hierarchical distinctions that often dictate whose work is regarded as "serious" and whose is not. Each surface becomes a conversation, a negotiation between history and the present, preservation and innovation.

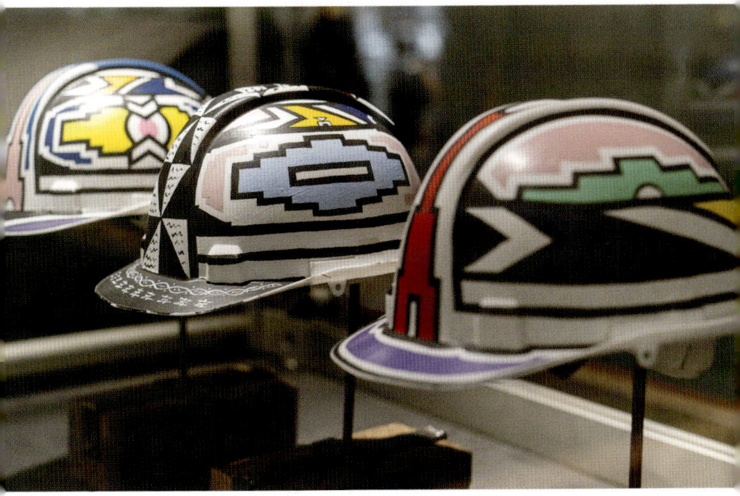

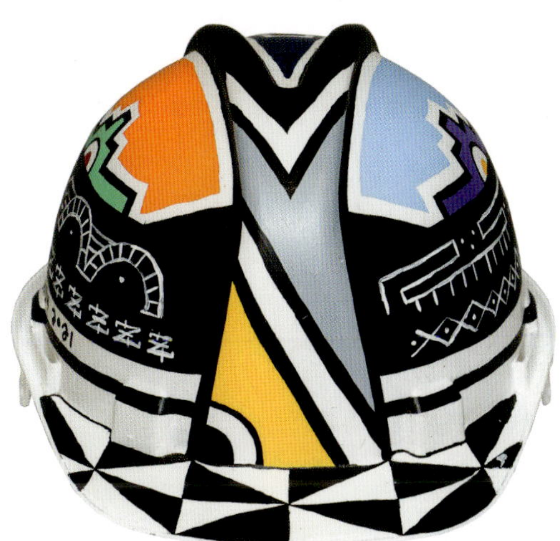

above
Installation view of painted miners' helmets in the exhibition *Then I Knew I Was Good at Painting: Esther Mahlangu, A Retrospective*, Wits Art Museum, Johannesburg, South Africa, 2024–2025

below
Miner's Helmet, 2021
Acrylic paint on miner's helmet
Dimensions unknown

Mahlangu's approach to surface is, in many ways, a testament to her understanding that art is not solely about what one sees but what one feels. Whether traced in the sand outside her studio or across a luxury car, her lines carry the weight of lived experience, a link to ancestral practices that ground her work and propel her artistic ideas forward. This ability to expand and sustain the integrity of her practice across a range of surfaces makes Mahlangu an innovator whose work defies categorization. Her power lies in her refusal to be confined—in her insistence that every surface, no matter how humble or prestigious, deserves the respect of her meticulous, unwavering hand.

"What many find interesting about my artworks is that although they are based on traditional Ndebele designs, they are still very modern and current."

Endnotes

1. Y-Jean Mun-Delsalle, "Esther Mahlangu, One of South Africa's Most Famous Artists, Perpetuates Traditional Ndebele Painting." Forbes, June 7, 2019. https://www.forbes.com/sites/yjeanmundelsalle/2019/06/07/esther-mahlangu-one-of-south-africas-most-famous-artists-perpetuates-traditional-ndebele-painting/
2. Mun-Delsalle, Forbes, June 7, 2019.

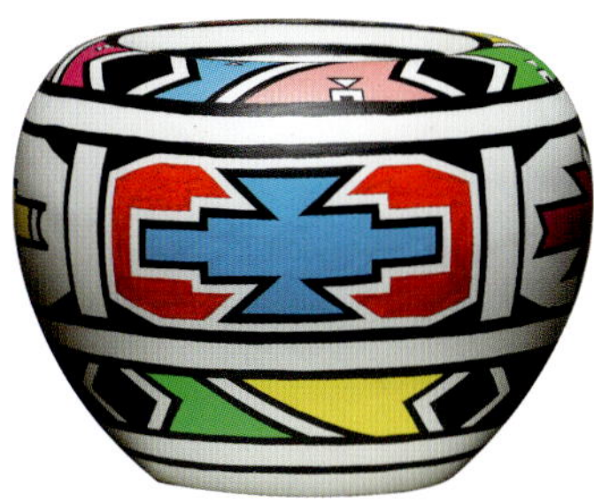

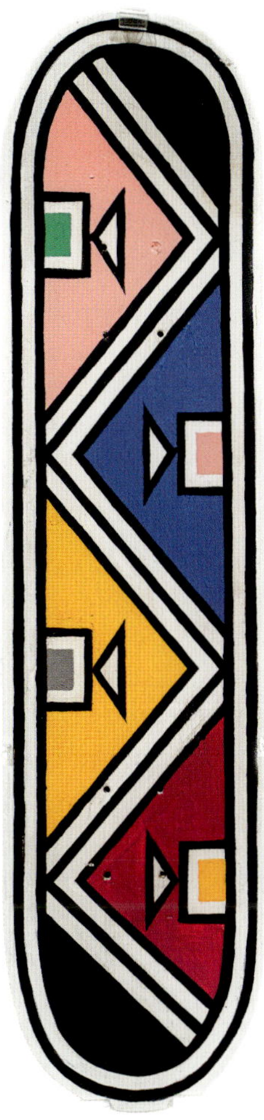

left
Skateboard Deck, 2016
Acrylic paint on skateboard
31 x 8 3/4 inches (79 x 20 cm)

above
Vessel, 2021
Acrylic paint on fiberglass container
11 $^3/_4$ inches x 15 $^3/_4$ diam. (30 x 40 cm)

below
Vessel, 2025
Acrylic paint on fiberglass container
31 $^1/_2$ inches x 15 $^3/_4$ diam. (80 x 40 cm)

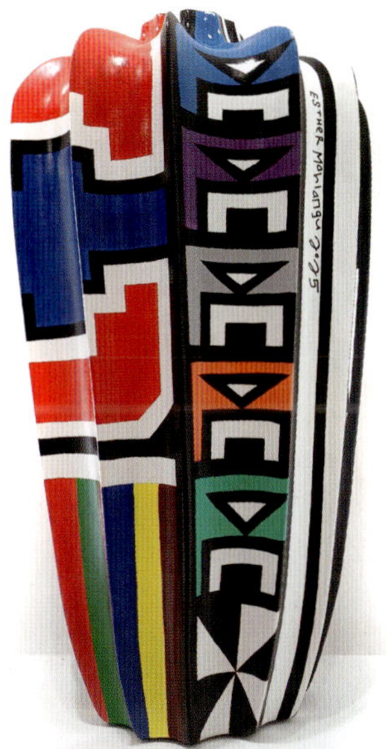

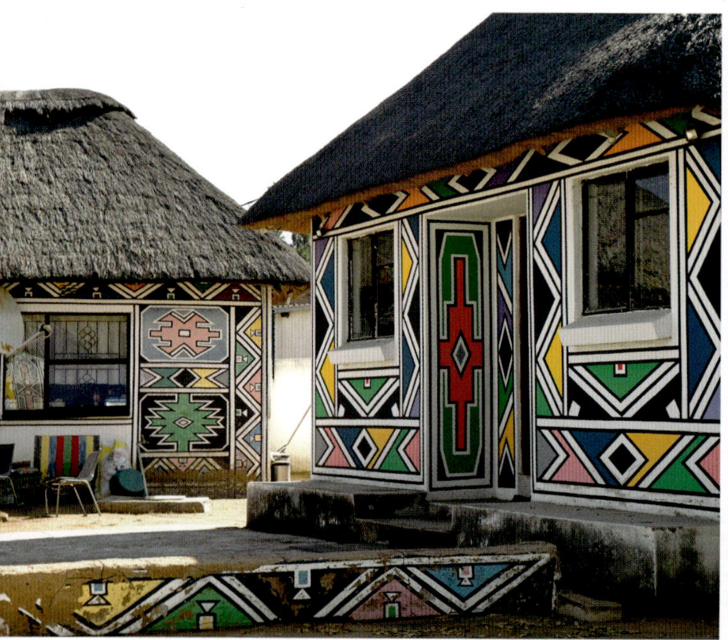

Esther Mahlangu's homestead in Mpumalanga, South Africa, 2023

"The well-known South African painter adapts Ndebele mural art for her large-scale geometric pictures . . . They're cheerful statement pieces that stand out in these gloomy times."

Wall Street Journal
May 2025

MAHLANGU & MURALS: A PATHWAY TO EXPRESSION

Esther Mahlangu's mural practice is the bedrock of her artistic journey. From a young age, she was taught the sacred art of painting the exterior walls of her family's home, a ritual that is both communal and profoundly personal. These murals represent a visual vernacular that marks identity, marks time, and celebrates life's milestones. As she mastered this practice, Mahlangu began to push the boundaries of her craft, envisioning how these traditional motifs could be adapted beyond their original context, yielding a new and expanded codex. This desire to expand the reach of Ndebele art set the stage for her transition from the walls of her village to the global art stage, where her work would come to adorn not just buildings but canvases, cars, and countless other surfaces. Years of experience painting façades instilled in her an acute understanding of how patterns can transform and animate a surface.

This strong foundation in mural painting uniquely prepared Mahlangu for her projects with other materials and diverse services, including the acclaimed 1991 BMW Art Car commission. For Mahlangu, the transition from mural to automobile was seamless. The expansive curves of the BMW 525i (page 65) became just another surface where her geometric mark-making could flow uninterrupted, wrapping the car in the same vibrant energy that had long adorned the walls of her community. Beyond decoration, the art car commission was about imbuing a modern industrial object with a

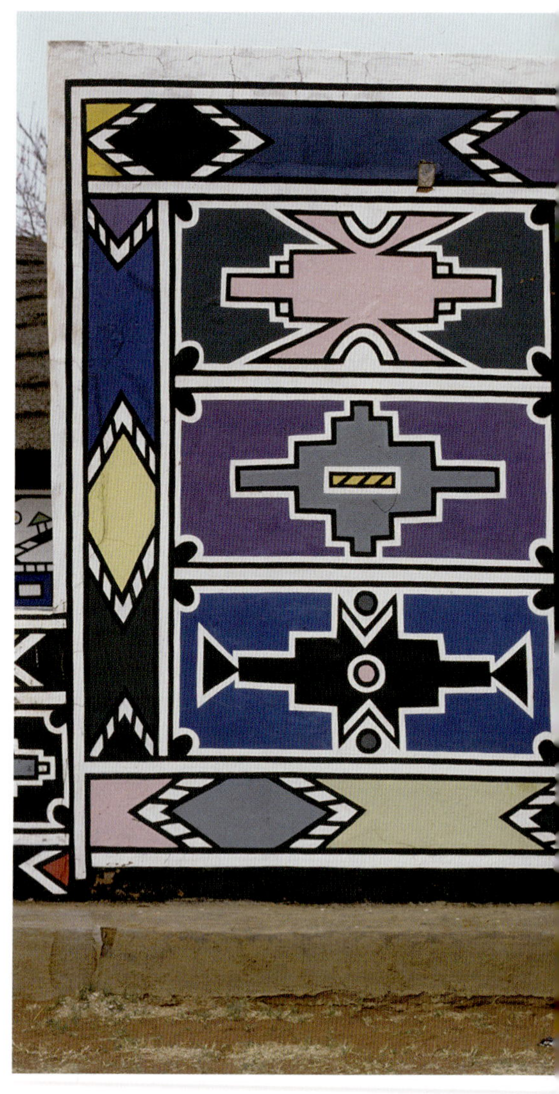

Mahlangu stands before one of her painted walls at Botshabelo Historical Village

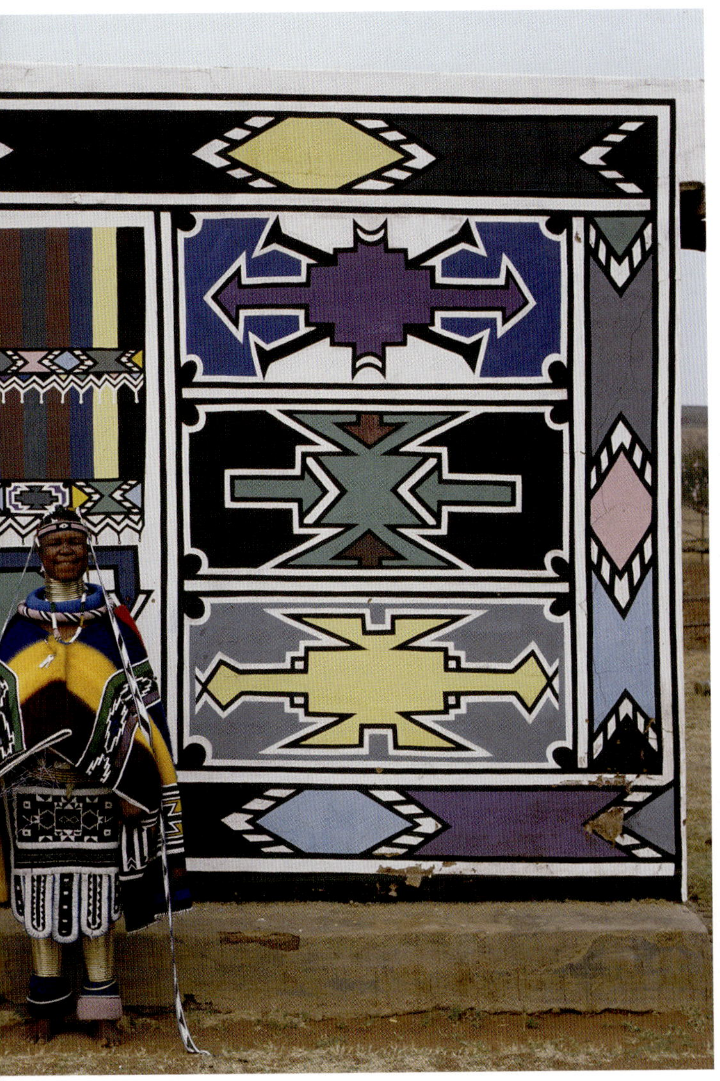

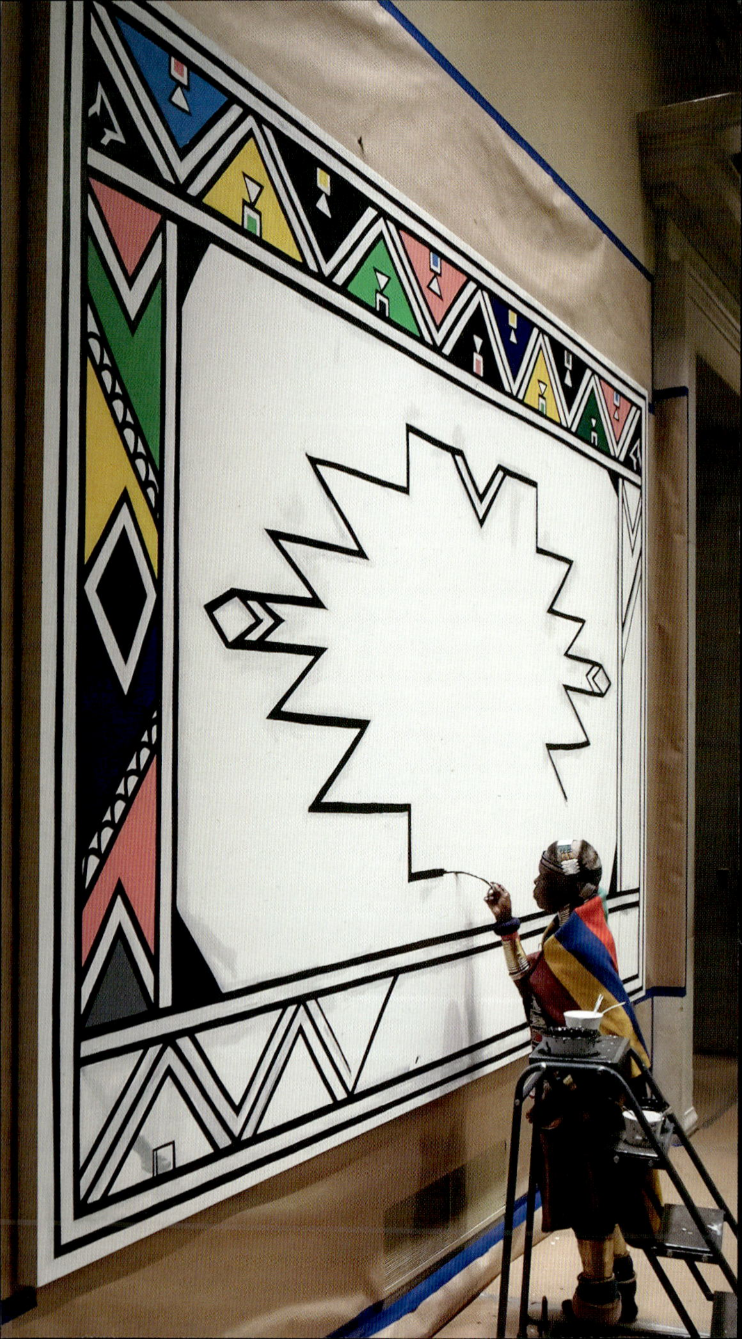

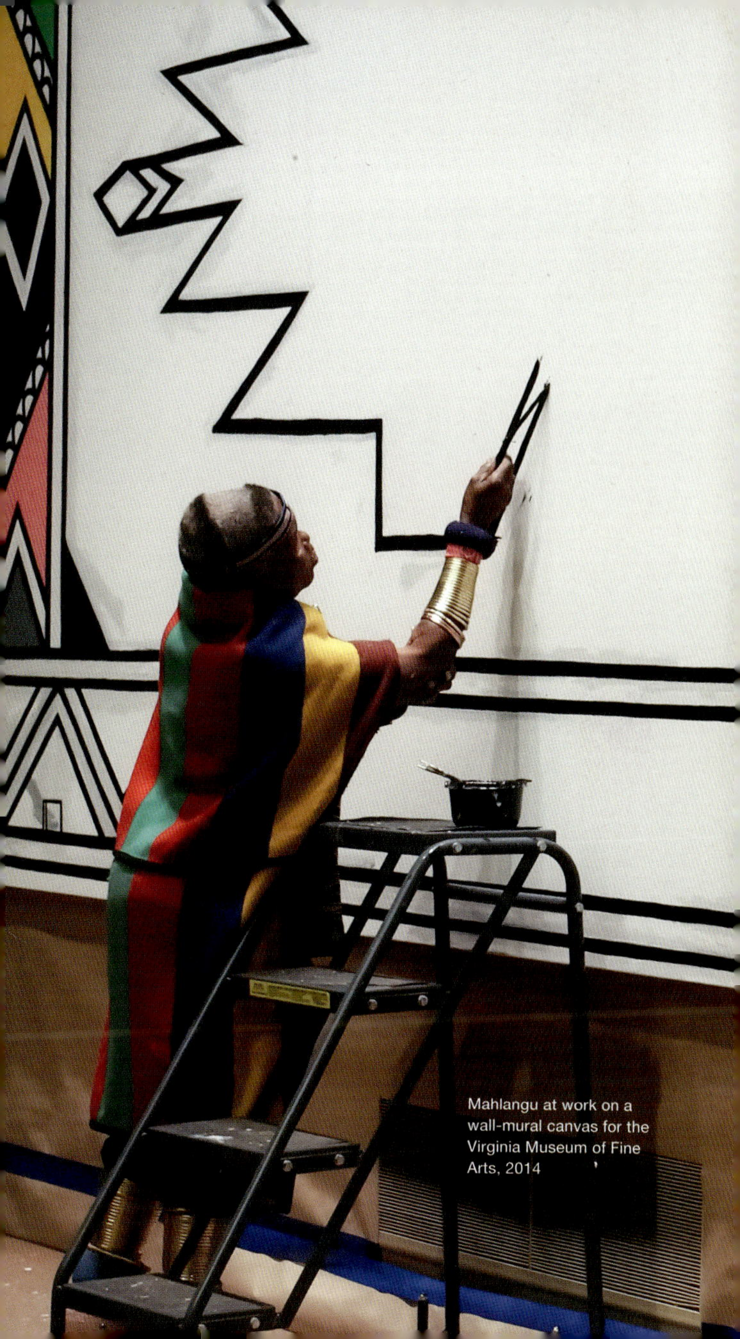

Mahlangu at work on a wall-mural canvas for the Virginia Museum of Fine Arts, 2014

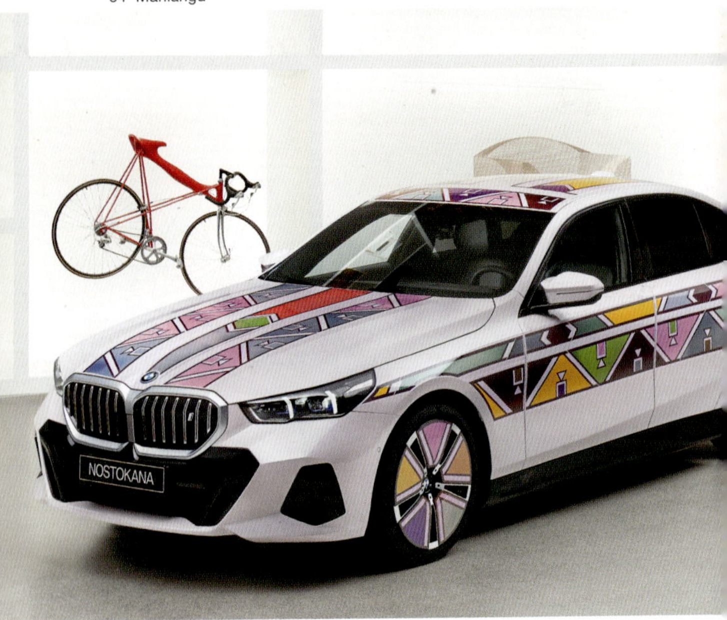

singular vision and artistic expression that was African, Indigenous, and from a female perspective.

What sets Mahlangu apart in her career is her obsession with painting all kinds of surfaces—an obsession that has become her signature. Whether it's the walls of a home, a canvas, a ceramic vase, a helmet, or a skateboard deck, Mahlangu approaches each surface with the same intensity and commitment. Her versatility has enabled her to continually innovate within her practice, adapting her visual vocabulary to new contexts and materials. This fearless exploration has kept her work dynamic and relevant. For Mahlangu, the surface is a space of endless possibility, where tradition meets experimentation.

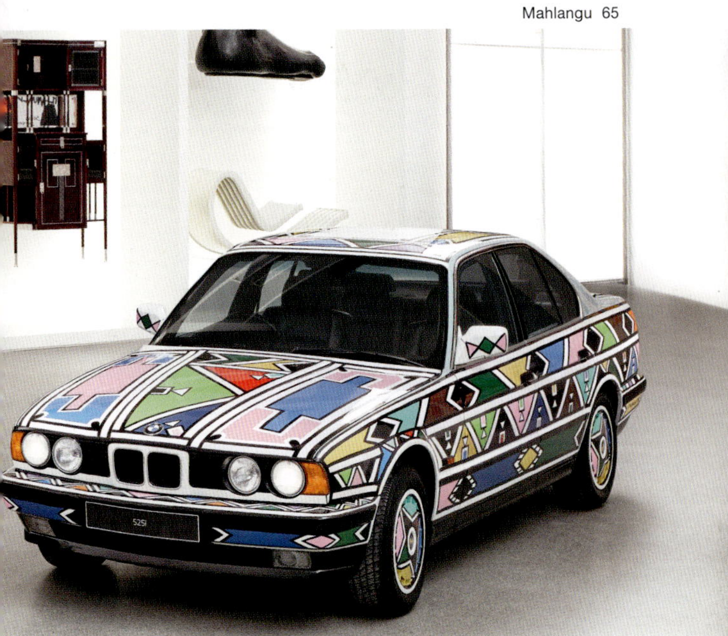

Her ability to translate the communal, ancestral art into a highly individual, contemporary vision—while maintaining its authenticity—has made her work both timeless and cutting-edge. Mahlangu's art reflects a tradition that is as much about innovation as preservation.

That zest for creative intervention has sparked some of Mahlangu's most notable recent projects. More than thirty years after her iconic art car commission, in 2023 she again collaborated with BMW—this time as one of five international artists whose art animations, developed by AI, were projected onto the surfaces of the new electric-powered i5.

At left, Mahlangu's latest Art Car for BMW, the AI-animated i5 *Flow Nostokana*, 2024; at right, her original Art Car, the 1991 BMW 525i

In January 2024, Mahlangu participated in Dhai Dubai, the first Emirati-led light and art festival in Dubai. This event brought together artists worldwide to transform the city's skyline with vibrant, large-scale light installations. As part of this festival, an immersive presentation of Mahlangu's work was projected on the interior walls and ceiling of an immense dome, enveloping viewers in her signature geometric patterns and vivid colors. The festival aimed to blend tradition with technology, and Mahlangu's work became a highlight. Her contribution stood out for its fusion of traditional cultural motifs with modern digital techniques, demonstrating how her art could seamlessly adapt to new forms of expression while preserving its essence.

For the installation, Mahlangu's patterns, often associated with the exterior of Ndebele homes, were projected in an animated sequence, creating a dynamic, pulsating environment that emphasized rhythm and movement. The interplay of light and shadow in this immersive setting allowed viewers to experience her work in a way that

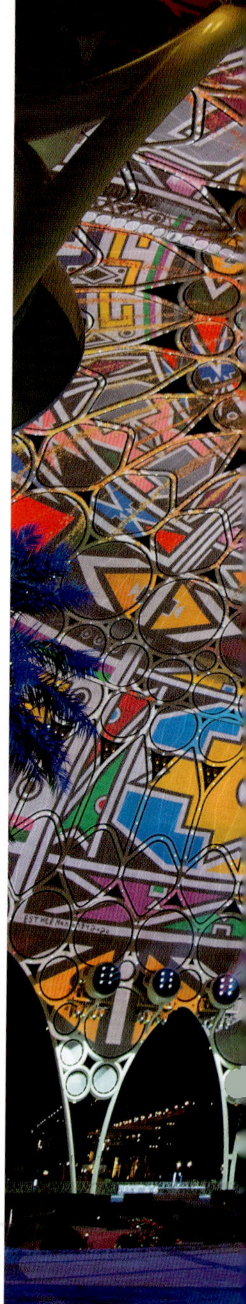

Mahlangu's *Sisters of the Desert* projection for Dhai Dubai 2024, presented at Al Wasi Plaza, Expo City Dubai

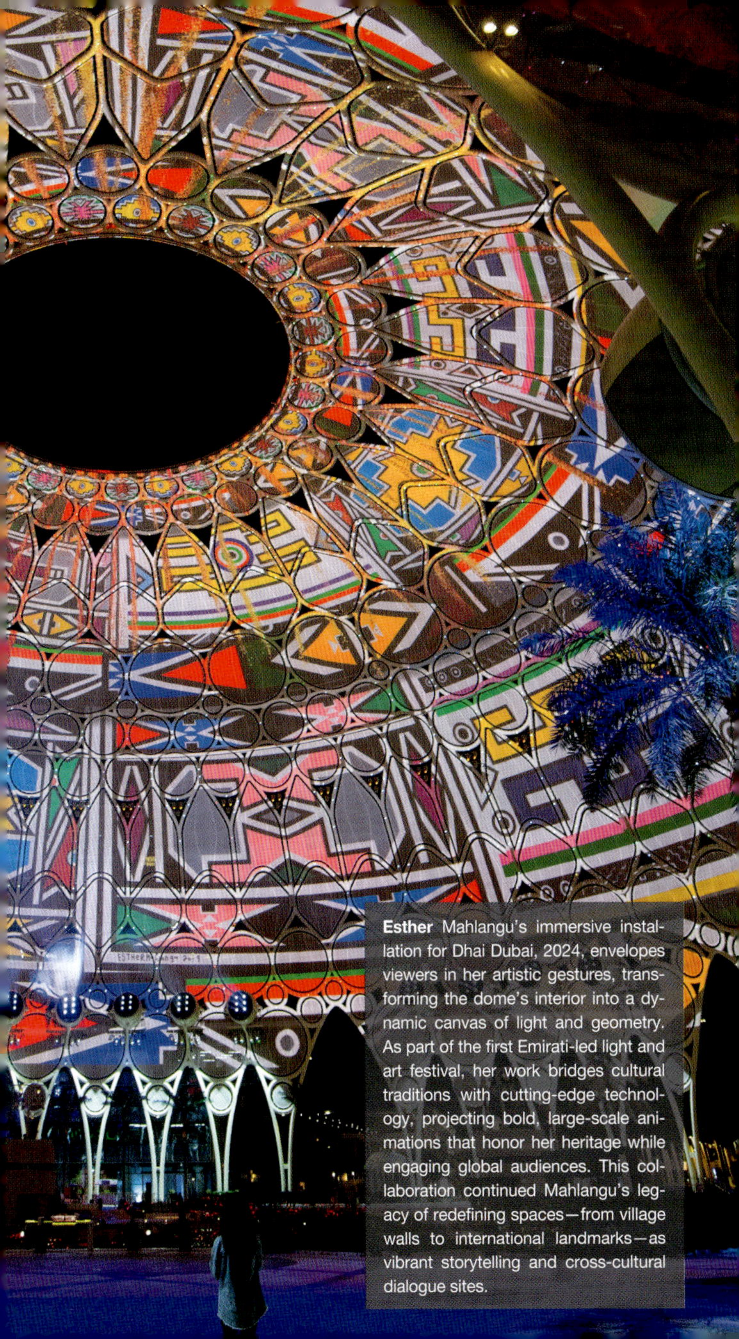

Esther Mahlangu's immersive installation for Dhai Dubai, 2024, envelopes viewers in her artistic gestures, transforming the dome's interior into a dynamic canvas of light and geometry. As part of the first Emirati-led light and art festival, her work bridges cultural traditions with cutting-edge technology, projecting bold, large-scale animations that honor her heritage while engaging global audiences. This collaboration continued Mahlangu's legacy of redefining spaces—from village walls to international landmarks—as vibrant storytelling and cross-cultural dialogue sites.

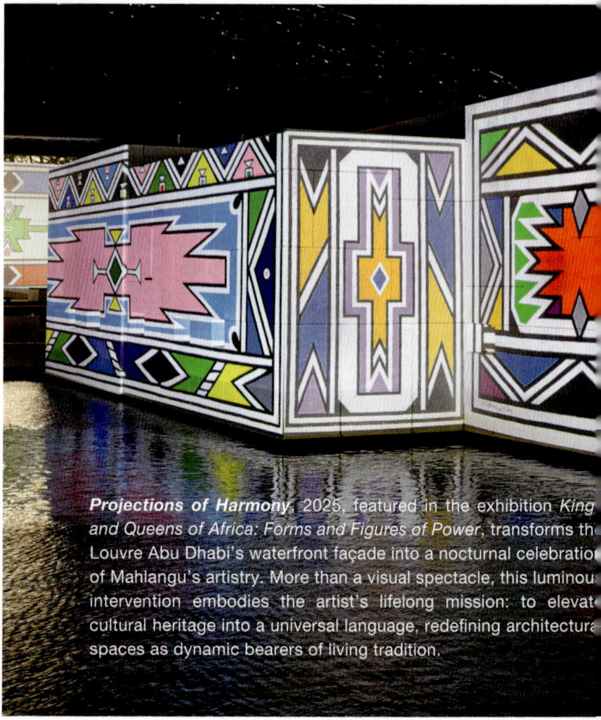

Projections of Harmony, 2025, featured in the exhibition *King
and Queens of Africa: Forms and Figures of Power*, transforms th
Louvre Abu Dhabi's waterfront façade into a nocturnal celebratio
of Mahlangu's artistry. More than a visual spectacle, this luminou
intervention embodies the artist's lifelong mission: to elevat
cultural heritage into a universal language, redefining architectura
spaces as dynamic bearers of living tradition.

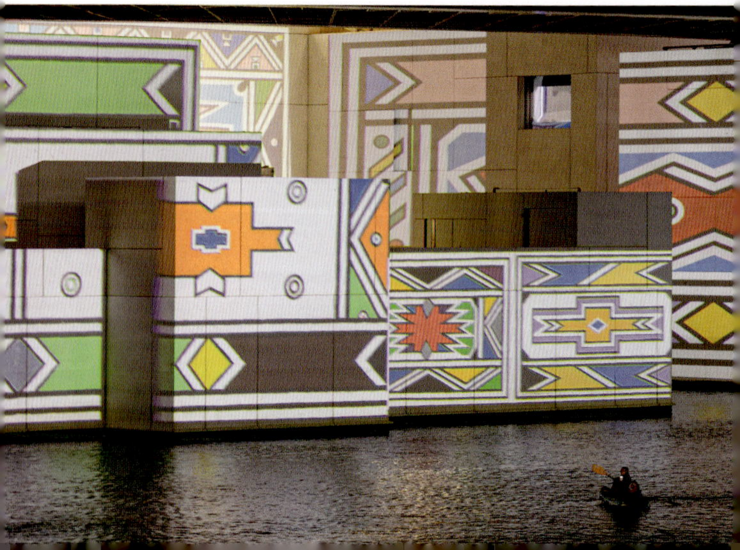

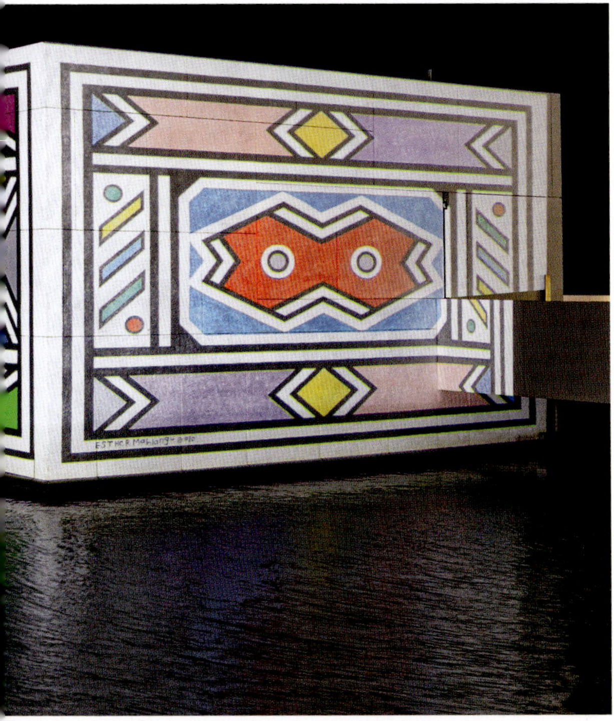

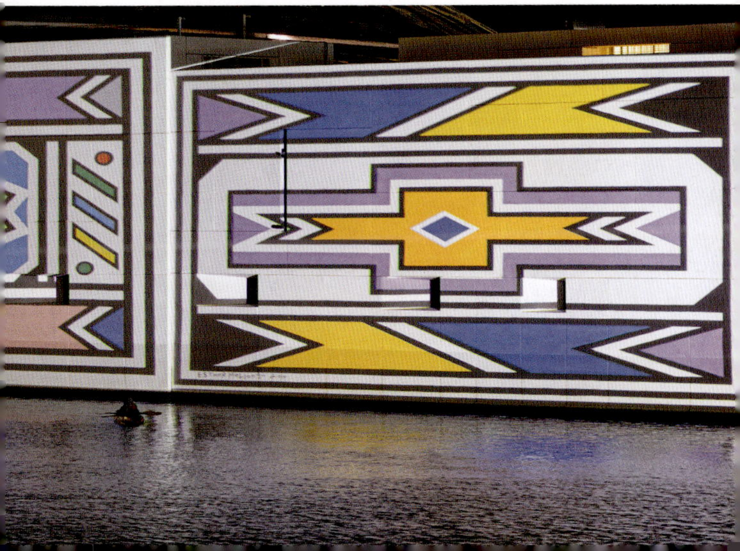

ESTHER Mahlangu 2010

ESTHER Mahlangu

transcended the two-dimensional surfaces she typically paints. This innovative fusion of light, art, and architecture offered a profound reflection on preserving cultural heritage and its continuous evolution in the digital age.

A year later, Mahlangu created a set of monumental light installations for the group exhibition *Kings and Queens of Africa: Forms and Figures of Power*, presented from January 29 to May 25, 2025, at the Louvre Abu Dhabi. Her suite of installations, titled *Projections of Harmony* (2025), illuminated the surfaces of the museum and were reflected in the surrounding waters.

Other aspects of Mahlangu's practice have also received increased attention. *Then I Knew I Was Good at Painting: Esther Mahlangu, A Retrospective,* opened in Cape Town at the Iziko South African National Gallery in 2024. It then traveled to the Wits Art Museum in Johannesburg, continuing into 2025. Curated by Nontobeko Ntombela, the exhibition celebrated seven decades of Mahlangu's artistic practice and featured over 100 works, offering an encompassing exploration of the depth and breadth of her career. In addition to showcasing her artistic achievements, the retrospective illuminated the cultural and historical significance of Mahlangu's work, contextualizing her contributions within the broader frameworks of Ndebele heritage and global contemporary art. The exhibition also emphasized her role as a cultural ambassador, highlighting her ability to translate traditional motifs into a universal visual language that resonates across borders.

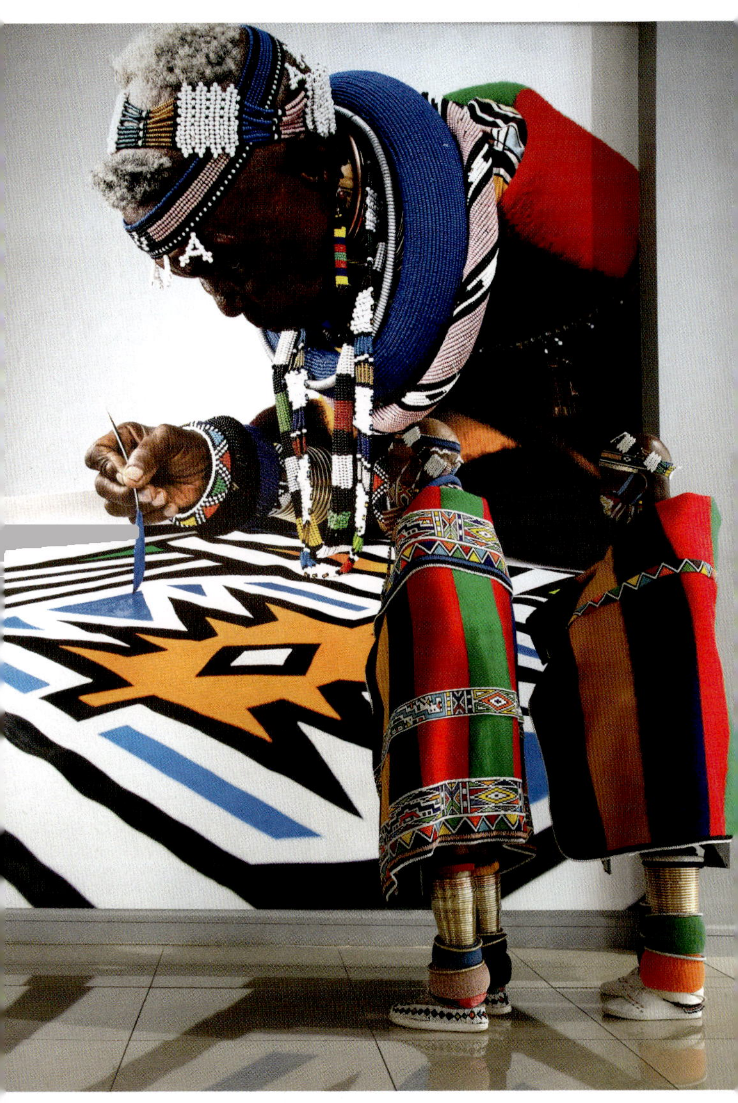

Mahlangu and a companion stand before her outsized image in the exhibition *Then I Knew I Was Good at Painting: Esther Mahlangu, A Retrospective* at the Iziko South African National Museum, Cape Town, 2024

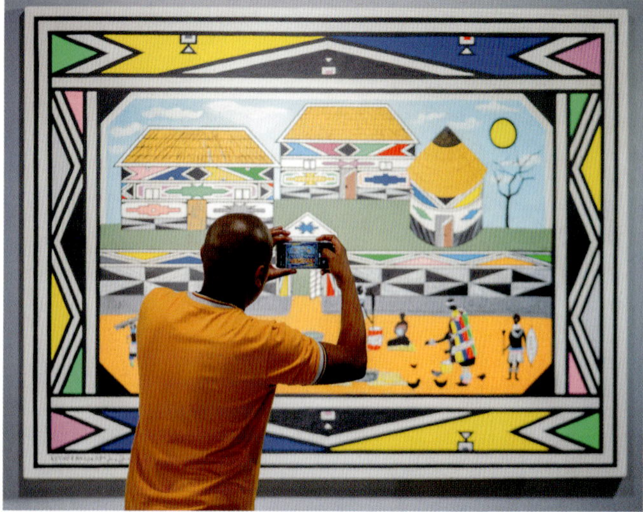

Through its comprehensive survey, *Then I Knew I Was Good at Painting* celebrated Mahlangu's enduring impact on art, culture, and the preservation of Indigenous knowledge systems, inspiring new generations of artists and audiences worldwide.

In October 2024, the Serpentine Gallery in London unveiled a monumental site-specific mural in the Serpentine North garden. The mural's title, *Umuntu ngumuntu ngabantu*, reflects Mahlangu's cultural heritage and her profound belief in the philosophy of interconnectedness. Translating as "I am because you are," the phrase is ingrained in the Ndebele ethos of Ubuntu, emphasizing community, mutual care, and the shared humanity that binds us all. Set in an expansive outdoor location in historic Hyde Park,

above and opposite
Viewers at the opening of *Esther Mahlangu 85*, an exhibition celebrating the artist's 85th birthday, which ran November 2020 to April 2021 at The Melrose Gallery, Johannesburg, South Africa

the mural showcases Mahlangu's bold use of geometric patterns and vivid colors and speaks to the historical and cultural ties between South Africa and the UK.

The mural's garden location imbues the artwork with a sense of harmony and exchange, connecting the urban landscape of London with the natural and spiritual elements of the Ndebele tradition. As Mahlangu herself said, "It is my wish that this painting brings much joy to those who see it in celebration and recognition of the interconnectedness that exists between our two nations and indeed all living beings."[1] Mahlangu continues her work of using art to bridge cultures and foster a deeper understanding of global unity through this large-scale public artwork.

Endnote
1. "Serpentine to Unveil Large-Scale Mural by Esther Mahlangu." Press release, Serpentine Gallery, London, September 19, 2024.

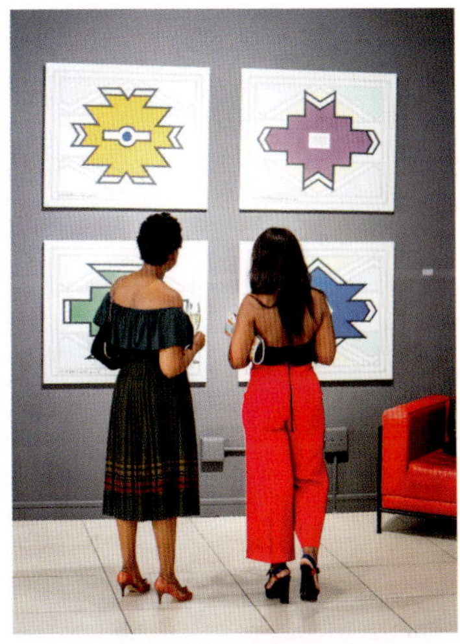

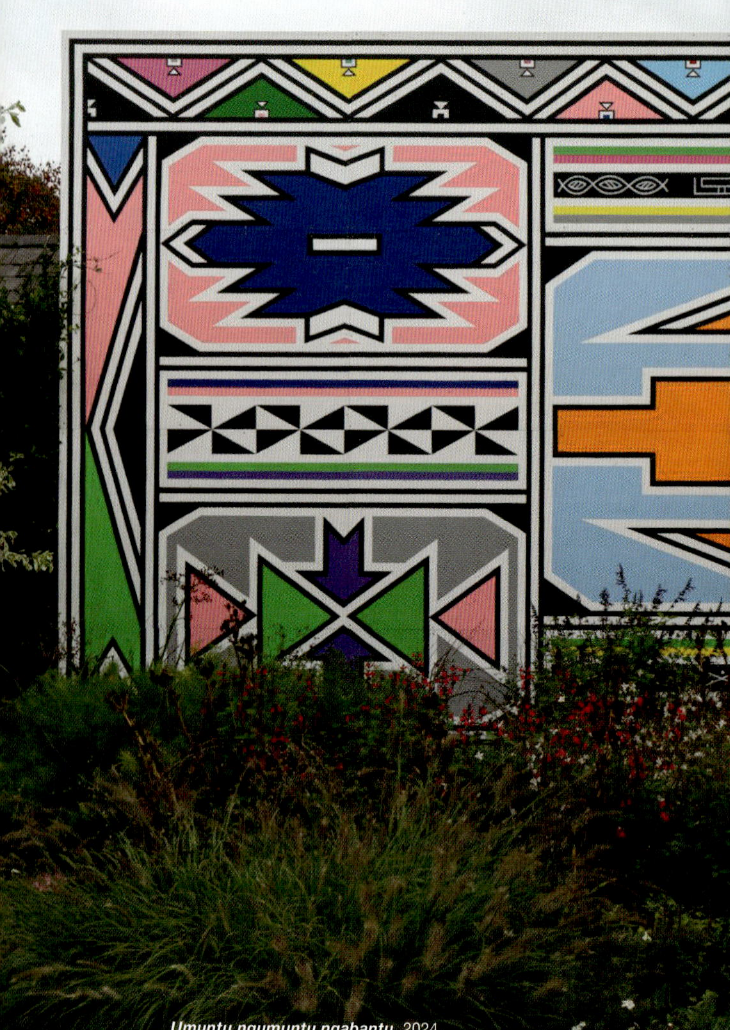

Umuntu ngumuntu ngabantu, 2024,
installed at the Serpentine Gallery, London
Acrylic paint on 16 wooden panels
354 x 197 inches (900 x 500 cm)

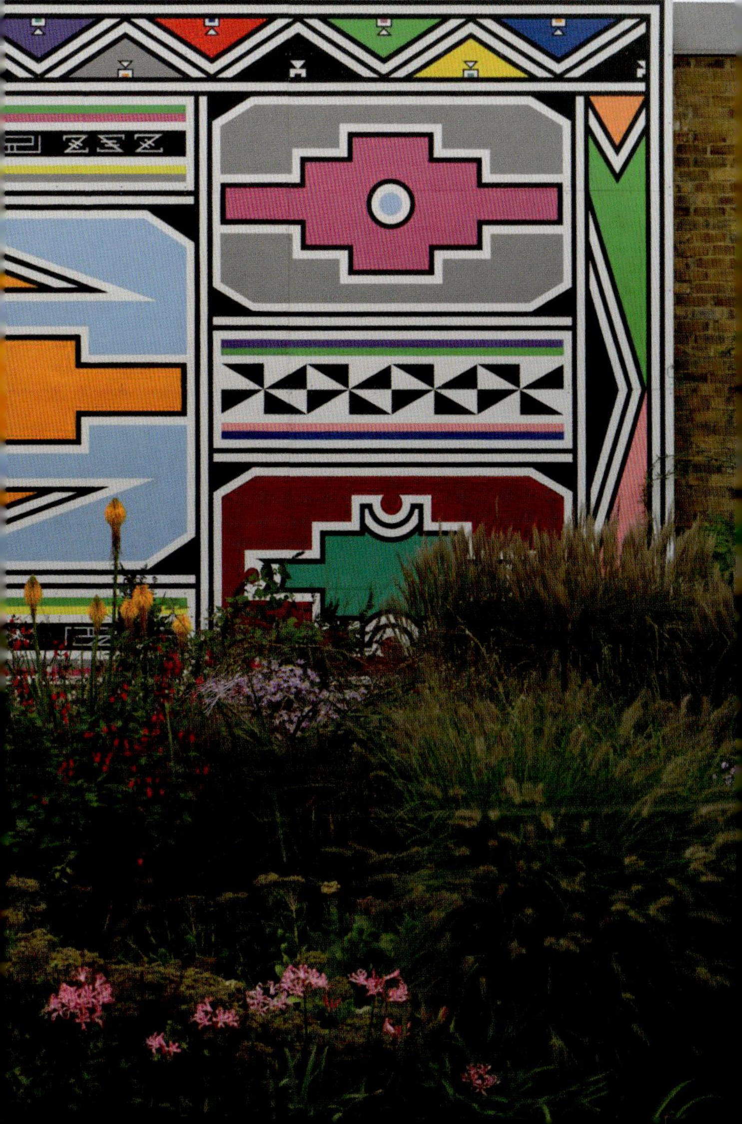

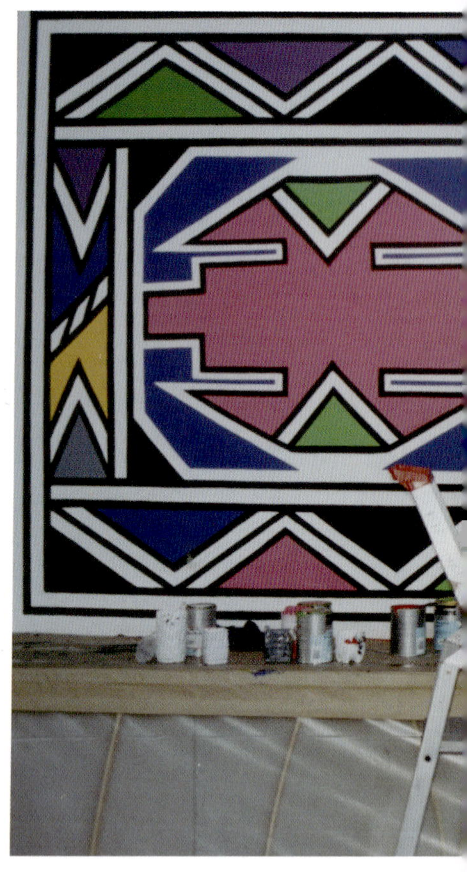

Mahlangu at work on *U'gwala*, 2000, the wall-sized work done in dialogue with a work by minimalist artist Sol LeWitt for the 5th Lyon Biennial, Lyon, France

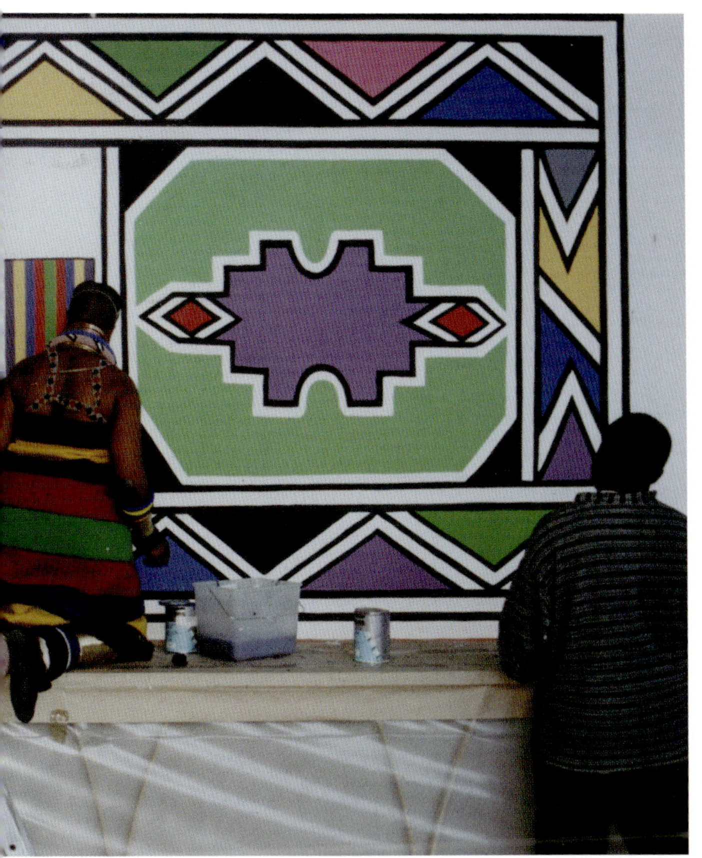

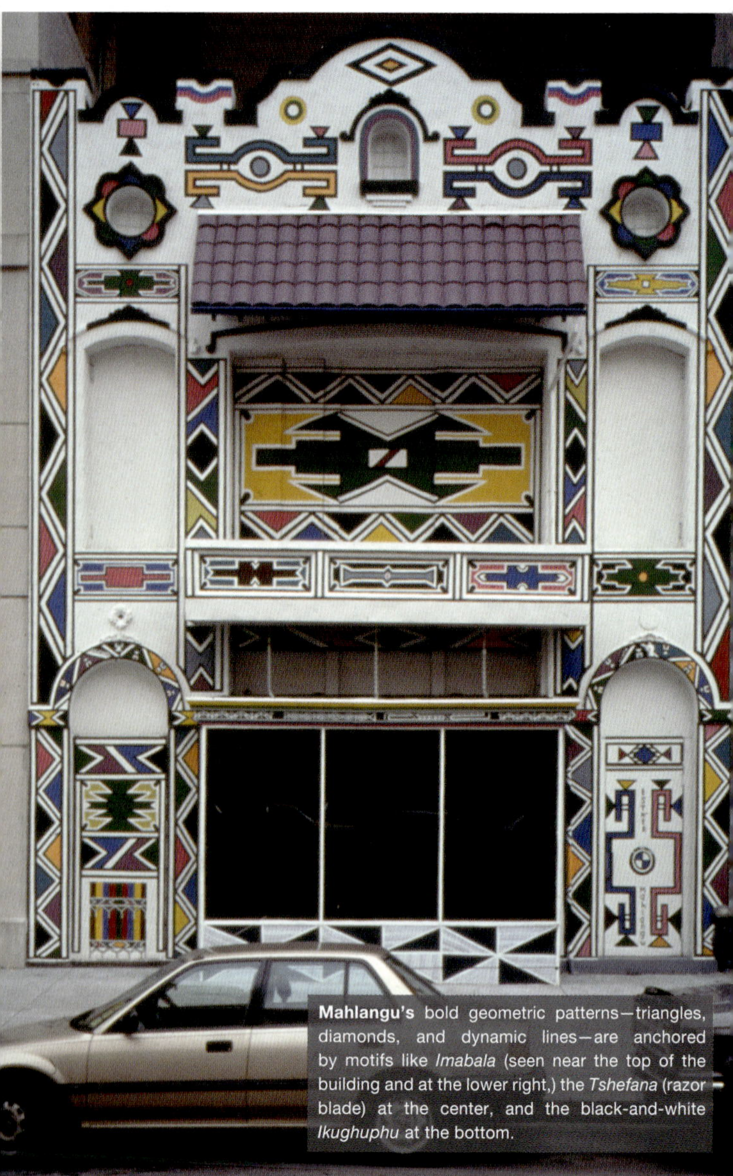

Mahlangu's bold geometric patterns—triangles, diamonds, and dynamic lines—are anchored by motifs like *Imabala* (seen near the top of the building and at the lower right,) the *Tshefana* (razor blade) at the center, and the black-and-white *Ikughuphu* at the bottom.

MAHLANGU & ARCHITECTURE

Esther Mahlangu's mastery in creating murals blurs the line between architectural surface and artistic expression. This connection to art and architecture has remained a defining feature of her practice throughout her career.

In many ways, Mahlangu's work can be seen as a dialogue between architecture and the natural environment. Her murals are often designed to coexist harmoniously with their surroundings, responding to the spatial dimensions of buildings and the broader landscape. The geometric motifs she employs—triangles, squares, diamonds—are not random patterns but are thoughtfully composed to echo the structural elements of architecture. Whether on the walls of homes in her native Mpumalanga province or contemporary galleries worldwide, they invoke a sense of rhythm and order that resonates with architectural principles. By transforming walls into vibrant canvases, she creates a visual interplay between the built environment and the natural world, honoring the Ndebele tradition of treating buildings as living entities.

Mahlangu's large-scale public artworks further her relationship with architecture and showcase her skill in activating space through her artistic practice. Her ability to adapt her art to monumental structures, whether on a

opposite
Mahlangu's installation on the façade of the National Museum of Women in the Arts, Washington, DC, 1994

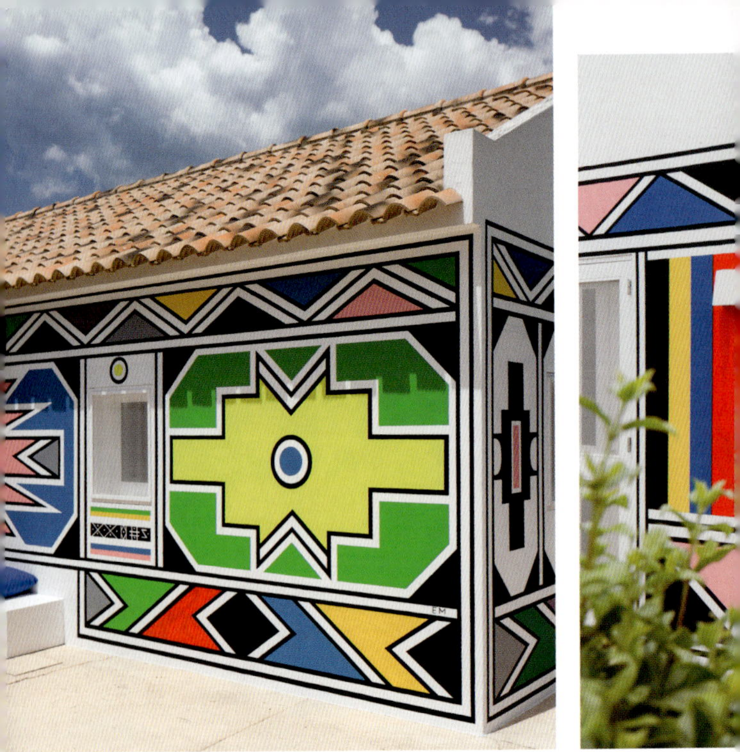

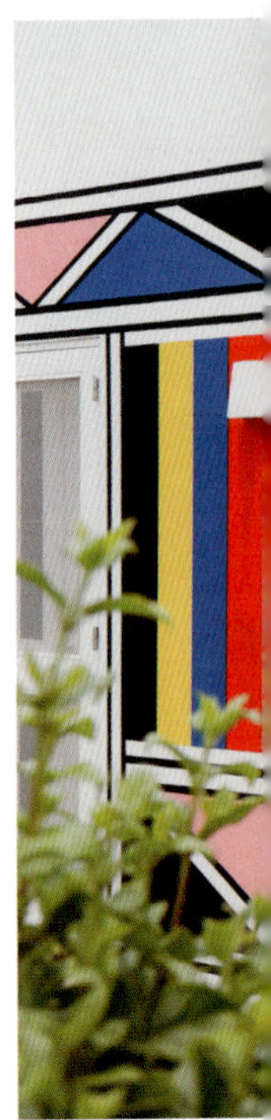

building's façade or in immersive installations, showcases her capacity to transcend cultural boundaries while maintaining a deep respect for her heritage. Notable examples include her striking mural work at the National Museum of Women in the Arts in Washington, DC, and the ambitious transformation of Casa Farida in Carvalhal, Portugal.

At Casa Farida, Mahlangu covered the façades of four traditional Portuguese fishermen's houses with over 1,400 square feet (430 square meters) of murals, blending her art with the architectural language of coastal Portugal. In

Two views of Mahlangu's façade art at Casa Farida
in Carvalhal, Portugual, 2022

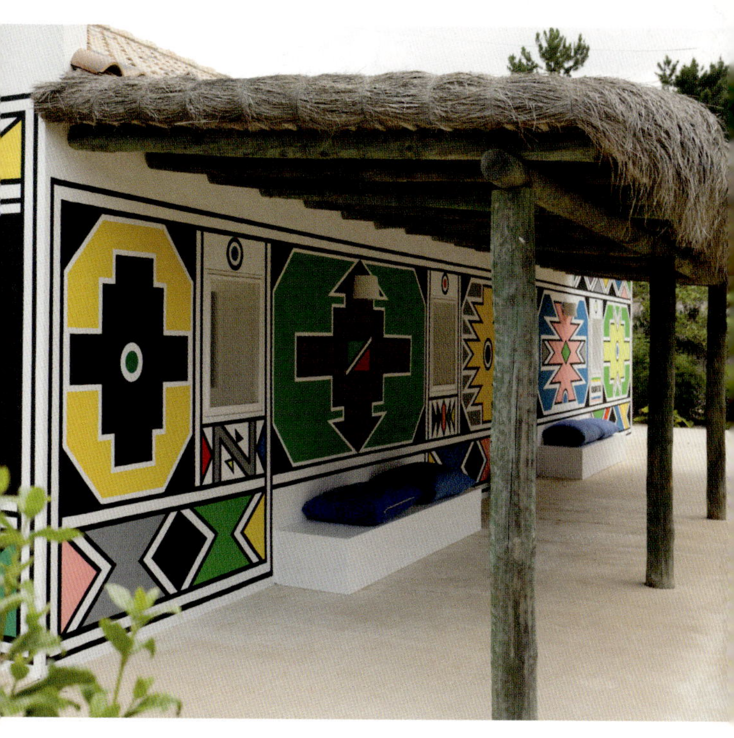

Gstaad, Switzerland, she adorned the spacious arrival area of a private residence. This project reflects her ability to adapt to diverse architectural contexts while maintaining the essence of her practice. These works position her art within global architectural spaces, inviting expansive conversations about how Indigenous and African contemporary art can engage with and transform modern architectural settings. In Mahlangu's work, architecture becomes both a canvas and a collaborator, emphasizing her belief in the interconnectedness of art, space, and community.

And yet, there is something else—a deeper intention threaded through each wall she transforms. When Mahlangu painted the façades of Casa Farida, her brush met surfaces made of lime and thatch, materials that have long absorbed the weight of coastal winds. The motifs she inscribed—symbols drawn from the earth itself, first traced in the sand—became meditative gestures, signals to a past and future interwoven in the present. Whether private homes or institutions, these structures hold within them not just her color and pattern but stories of migration, labor, and belonging. Her architectural interventions are acts of reclamation, marking territory in a world where the boundaries of visibility and power constantly shift. The buildings she adorns become witnesses to her vision, bearing the evidence of a woman whose artistry both embodies and defies categorization.

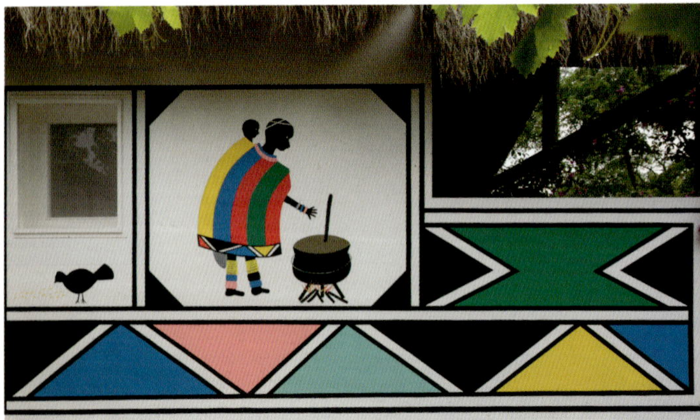

Two views of Mahlangu's façade art at Casa Farida in Carvalhal, Portugual, 2022. Although her art is primarily geometric, Mahlangu occasionally portrays figurative scenes like the one here.

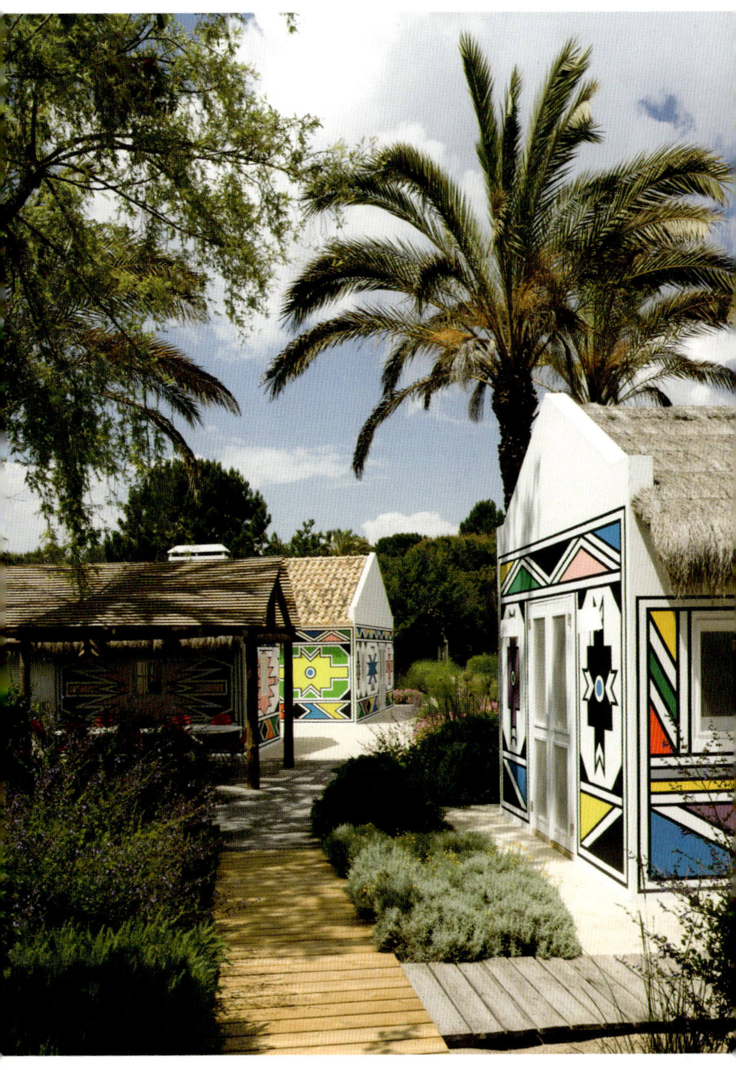

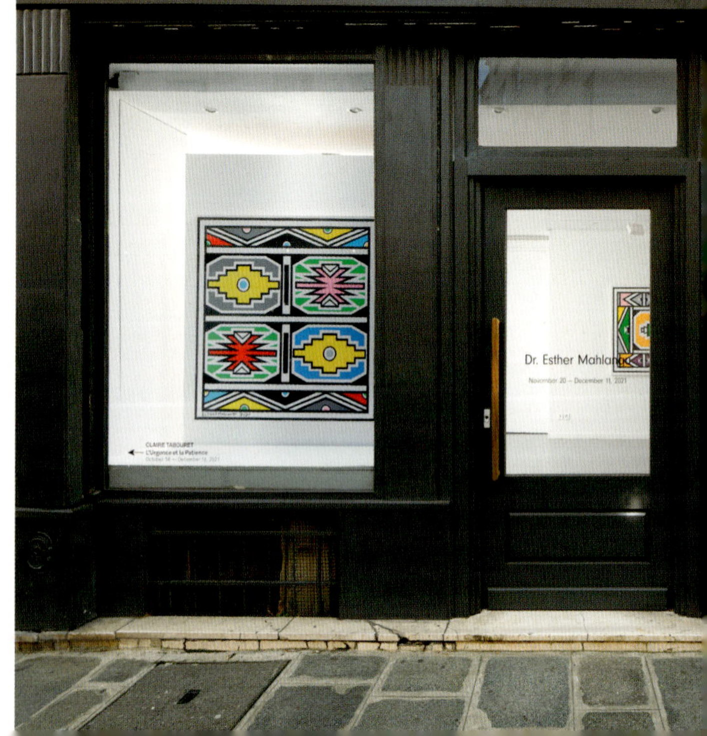
CLAIRE TABOURET
L'Urgence et la Patience
October 16 — December 11, 2021
Dr. Esther Mahlangu
November 20 — December 11, 2021

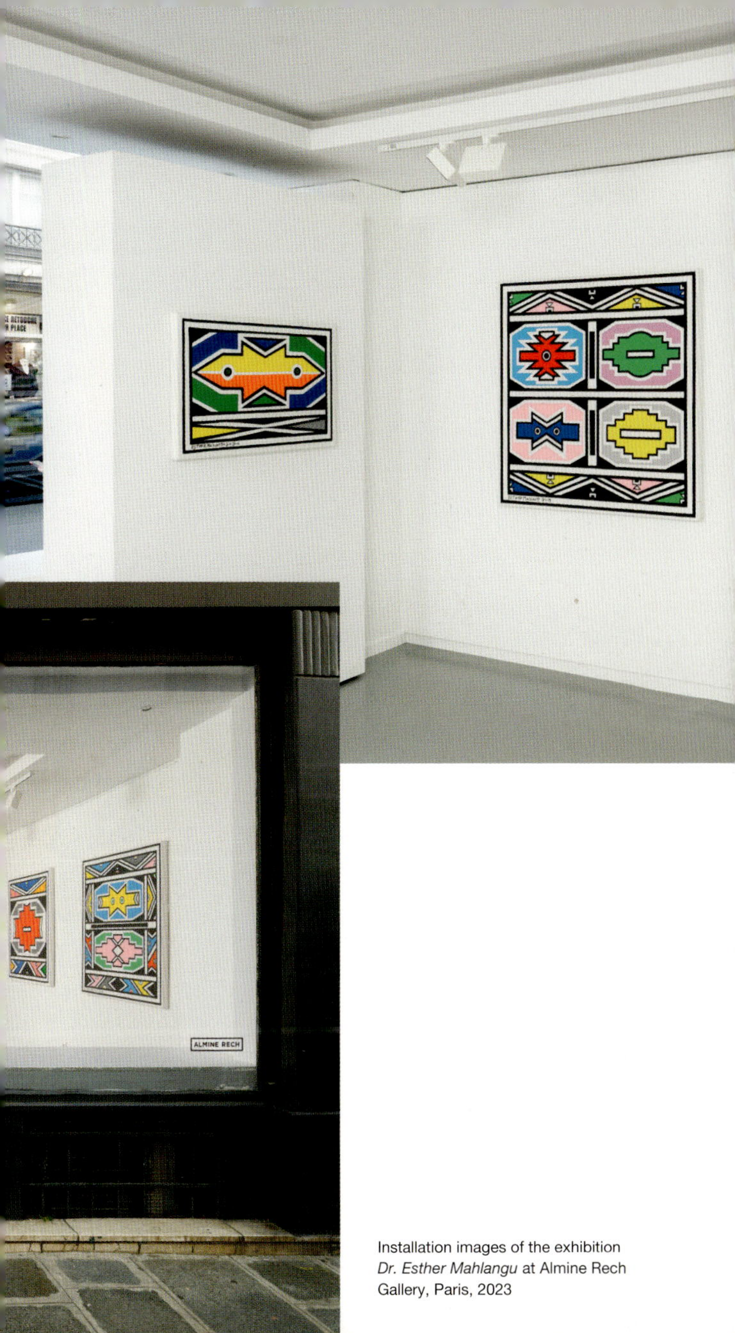

Installation images of the exhibition
Dr. Esther Mahlangu at Almine Rech
Gallery, Paris, 2023

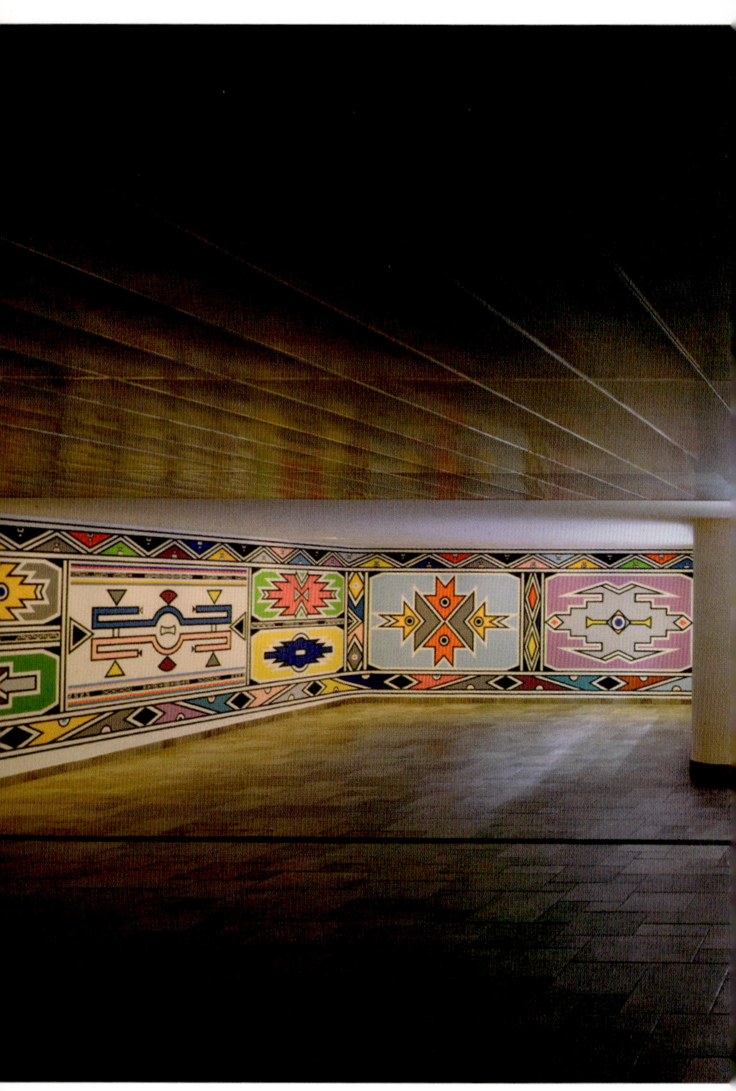

The arrival area for a private residence in Gstaad, Switzerland, featuring
large-scale murals by Esther Mahlangu, 2025

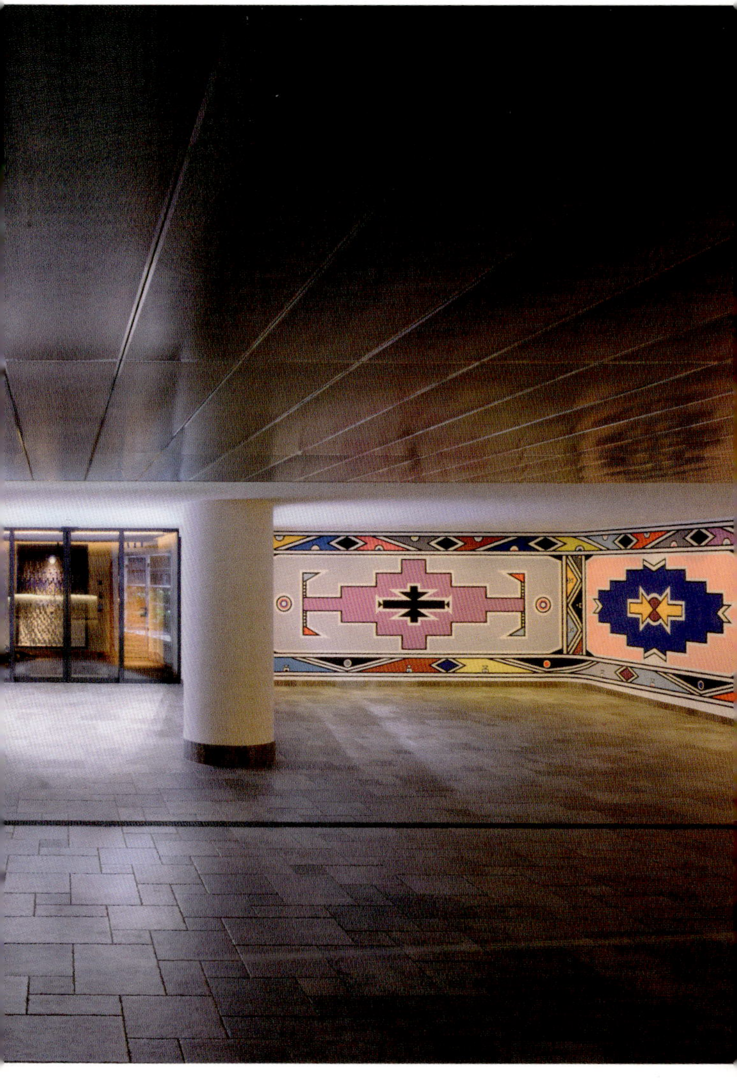

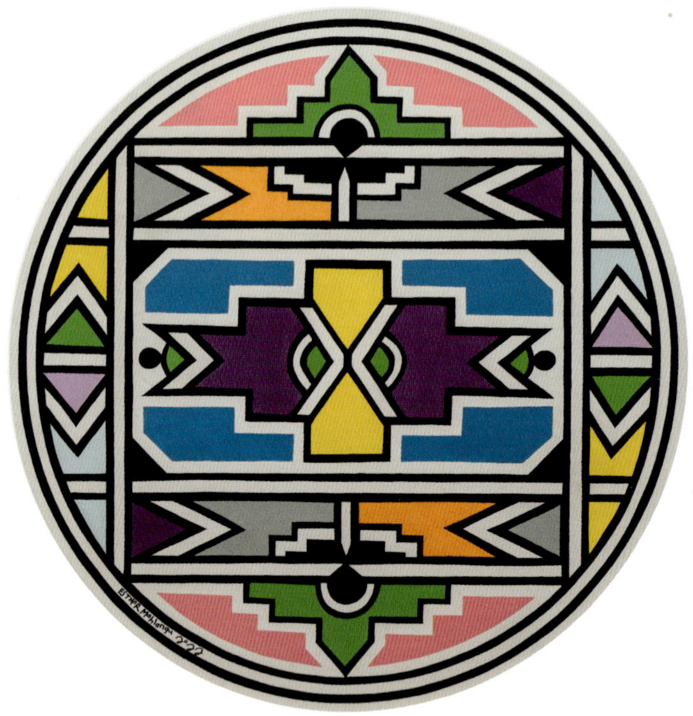

Ndebele Abstract, 2022
Acrylic paint on canvas
70 inches (180 cm) in diameter

A VISUAL TÉTE-À-TÉTE: MAHLANGU AND OTHER ARTISTS

To fully appreciate Esther Mahlangu's work, it is helpful to contextualize her practice alongside several other international artists—specifically, Lygia Clark, Jeffrey Gibson, Carmen Herrera, Sol LeWitt, Alma Thomas, and Stanley Whitney. Placing Mahlangu's work in conversation with these artists reveals a shared language of geometric abstraction, color, and form that transcends cultural and geographical boundaries. While each artist is entrenched in distinct traditions and contexts, they all explore the universal possibilities of abstraction, expanding our understanding of how color, line, and shape can convey complex ideas and emotions.

Mahlangu's vibrant, rhythmic patterns resonate with the conceptual clarity of LeWitt's wall drawings, the precise formalism of Herrera's compositions, and the expressive geometry of Thomas's and Whitney's canvases. These connections reveal how Mahlangu's work, like the work of these artists, challenges the often Western-centric narrative of abstraction. Like their work, Mahlangu's art asserts a vital place for Indigenous practices in the broader discourse of contemporary art, demonstrating that abstraction is a shared language with diverse and vibrant expressions worldwide.

These artists also share a profound understanding of how abstraction can transform space, whether it's the walls of a gallery, the streets of a city, or the surface of a canvas. LeWitt's expansive wall works, like Mahlangu's murals, turn architectural space into a dynamic field of visual engagement. Whitney and Mahlangu harness color's power to create a sense of movement and balance, while Gibson and Thomas use geometric forms to meld cultural heritage with contemporary aesthetics. Exploring these parallels, we can see more clearly how Esther Mahlangu's practice is a vital contribution to the global conversation on abstraction, color, and form. These dialogues illuminate how her work stands toe to toe with these celebrated figures, enriching our understanding of the interconnectedness of artistic practices across different cultures and eras.

What distinguishes Mahlangu is her ability to honor tradition while simultaneously reinventing it. Her work embodies a fluidity that navigates between the ancestral and the contemporary—similar to how Gibson integrates his Native North American heritage into his bold, modern pieces or Thomas reinterprets natural forms through an abstract lens. Mahlangu's patterns are rooted in cultural practices yet continuously evolving, and they are in kinship with Whitney's improvisational grids, Herrera's disciplined lines, and Clark's innovative exploration of sensory engagement. These comparisons situate Mahlangu within a wide-ranging lineage of geometric abstraction.

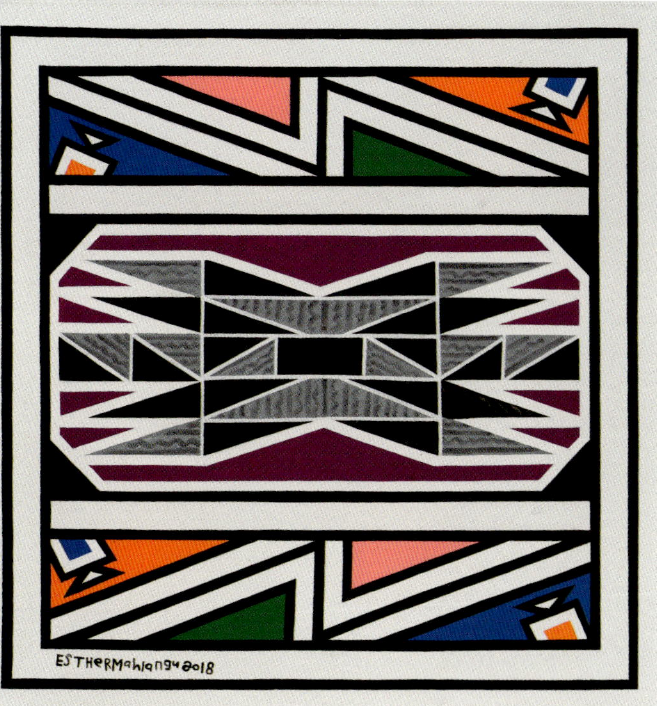

Untitled (Ndebele Abstract), 2018
Acrylic paint on canvas
47 x 47 inches (119.4 x 119.4 cm)

Esther Mahlangu and Sol LeWitt

A pioneer of conceptual art and minimalism, Sol LeWitt (1928–2007) is known for his radical approach to wall drawings, in which the idea is the art. In these works, LeWitt's directions, executed by others, produce striking works based on simple, repetitive geometric forms. Mahlangu and LeWitt share a profound understanding of space, which they explore through their respective practices. This shared vision was notably highlighted at the 5th Lyon Biennial (2000), where their works were set in conversation on a single wall.

Both artists use repetition and geometry to create an expansive sense of space beyond the physical surface. While LeWitt's work often explores conceptual possibilities, Mahlangu's patterns achieve a similar universality, asserting that the wall—whether in a gallery or a public space—is a site for intellectual and cultural engagement. The visual dialogue between their works at the Lyon Biennial is a testament to their unique yet related artistic languages.

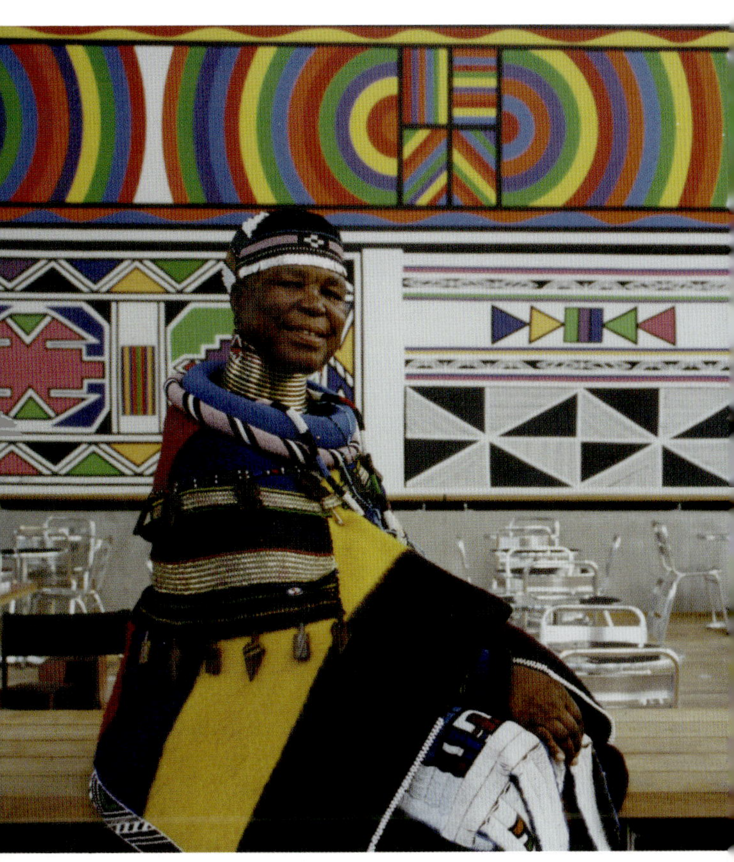

Esther Mahlangu seated before her mural *U'gwala*, 2000, presented in dialogue with *Wall Work #947* by minimalist artist Sol LeWitt, installed just above Mahlangu's work at the 5th Lyon Biennial, Lyon, France, 2000.

Esther Mahlangu and Carmen Herrera

Much like Mahlangu, Carmen Herrera (1915–2022)—a Cuban-born artist celebrated for her precise geometric abstractions—gained significant recognition late in life. Mahlangu's engagement with space parallels Herrera's, in which line, shape, and color are meticulously calculated to achieve a harmonious balance. Both artists have a deep sensitivity to how their compositions interact with the spaces they occupy. Much like Herrera's large-scale works, Mahlangu's murals command the viewer's attention, making the space they inhabit an integral part of the experience. Both artists challenge the viewer to reconsider the relationship between art and environment, demonstrating that abstraction is not just a matter of form but of how those forms transform our perception of space.

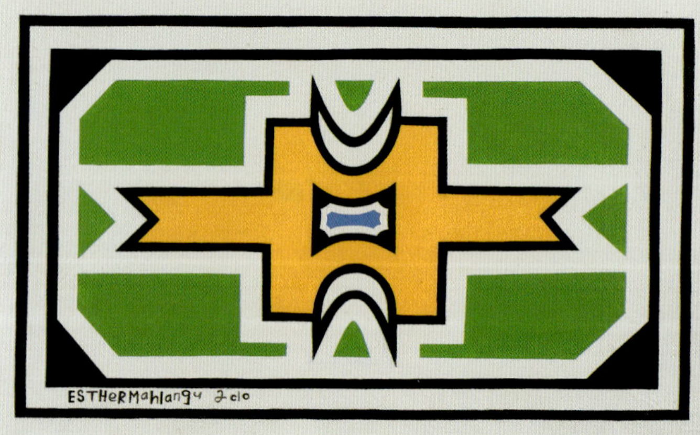

Untitled (Ndebele Abstract), 2010
Acrylic paint on canvas
22 x 38 inches (55 x 95.5 cm)

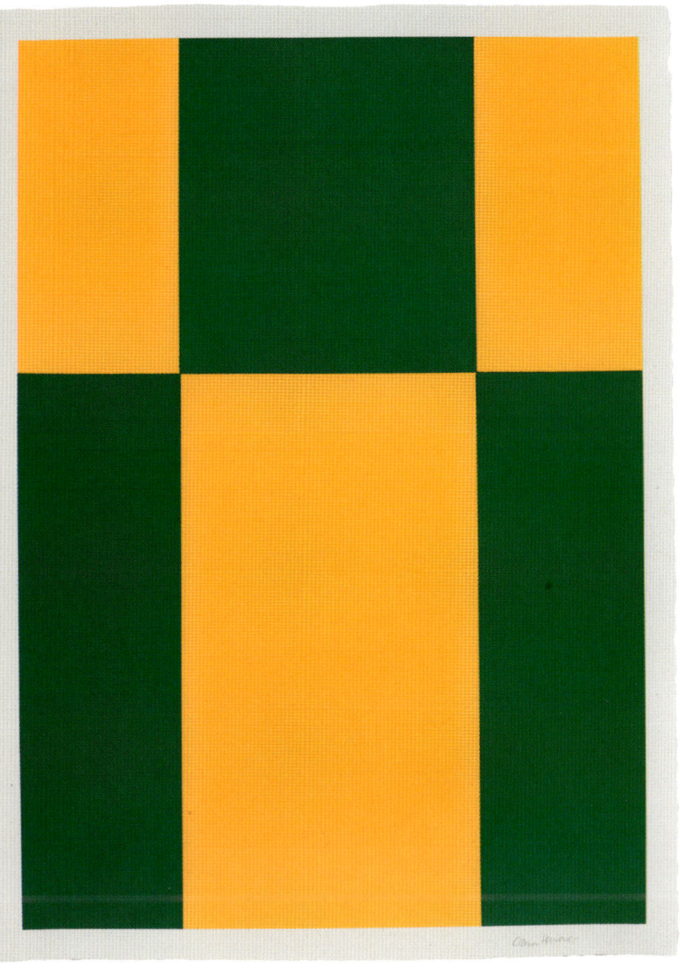

Carmen Herrera
Untitled, 2016
Acrylic on paper
29 $^7/_8$ x 23 $^1/_2$ inches (75.9 x 59.7 cm)

Esther Mahlangu and Jeffrey Gibson

The work of both Jeffrey Gibson (b. 1972), an American interdisciplinary artist of Choctaw and Cherokee descent, and Esther Mahlangu exemplifies the power of Indigenous art to speak across time and space, existing within a continuum that blends ancestral traditions with modern expression. Gibson's works often create environments where Native North American motifs merge with diverse mediums and popular culture, transforming space into a living narrative. "I may be a DJ visual remixer," he has said, "but I didn't invent appliqué. I didn't invent rickrack; I didn't invent beadwork. I see myself as a continuation of these things that have existed before me."[1] Like Gibson, Mahlangu demonstrates that Indigenous artists are not confined to history and their work exists within and beyond the contemporary canon. Their art confronts the notion of space as passive, instead using it as a medium through which identity is continually redefined.

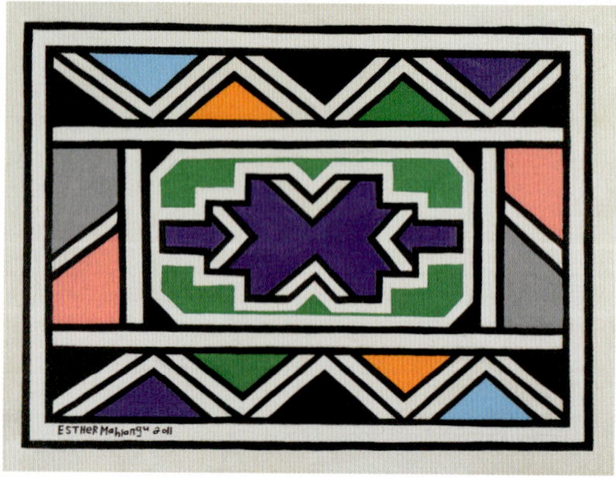

Untitled (Ndebele Abstract), 2011
Acrylic paint on canvas
34 x 47 1/4 inches (86 x 120 cm)

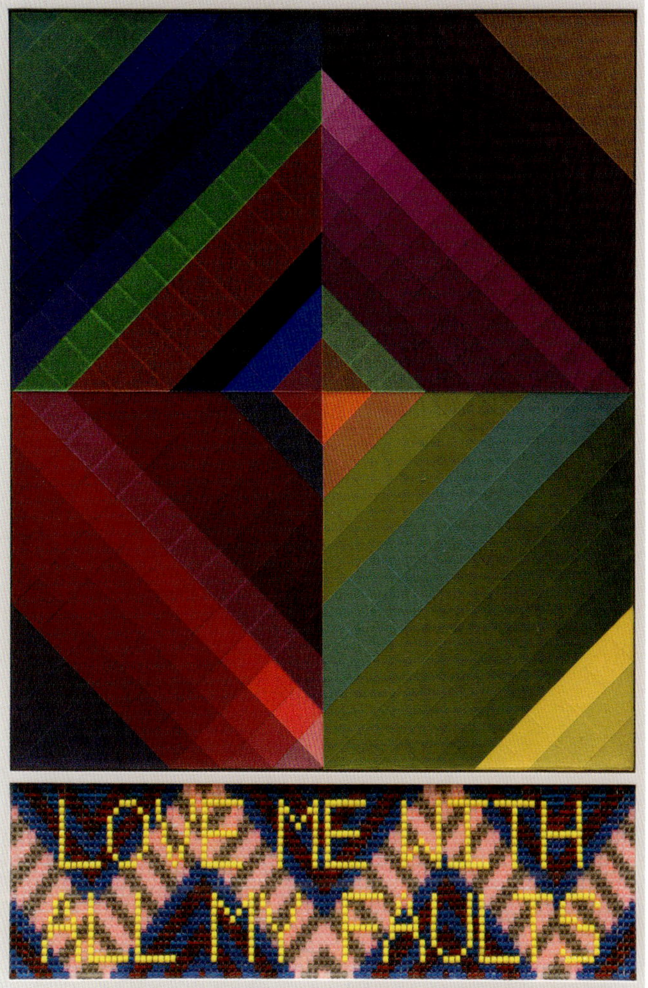

Jeffrey Gibson
LOVE ME WITH ALL MY FAULTS, 2023
Acrylic on canvas, glass beads, artificial sinew set into custom wood frame
44 x 39 inches (111.8 x 99.1 cm)

Esther Mahlangu and Stanley Whitney

Stanley Whitney (b. 1946) is an acclaimed African American abstract painter known for vibrant compositions based on loose, improvisational grids. Like Mahlangu, Whitney is deeply committed to exploring color and structure. With their syncopated blocks of color, his signature grids call to mind the visual harmony in Mahlangu's geometric patterns. Both artists understand how varying color combinations create balance and tension within a given space. Mahlangu's mark-making, with its bold lines and vibrant hues, resonates with the sense of order and improvisation that characterizes Whitney's work. Each artist transforms abstract shapes into a language of personal and cultural expression. Their works express a shared comprehension that color and form are not just decorative elements but vital tools for conveying meaning and emotion.

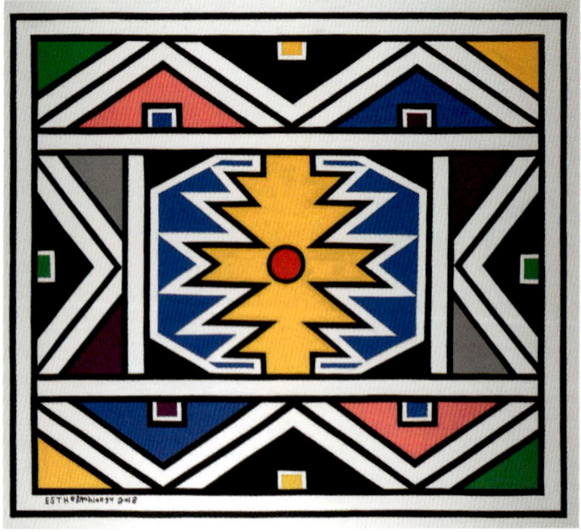

Untitled (Ndebele Abstract), 2018
Acrylic paint on canvas
71 ³/₄ x 63 inches (180 x 160 cm)

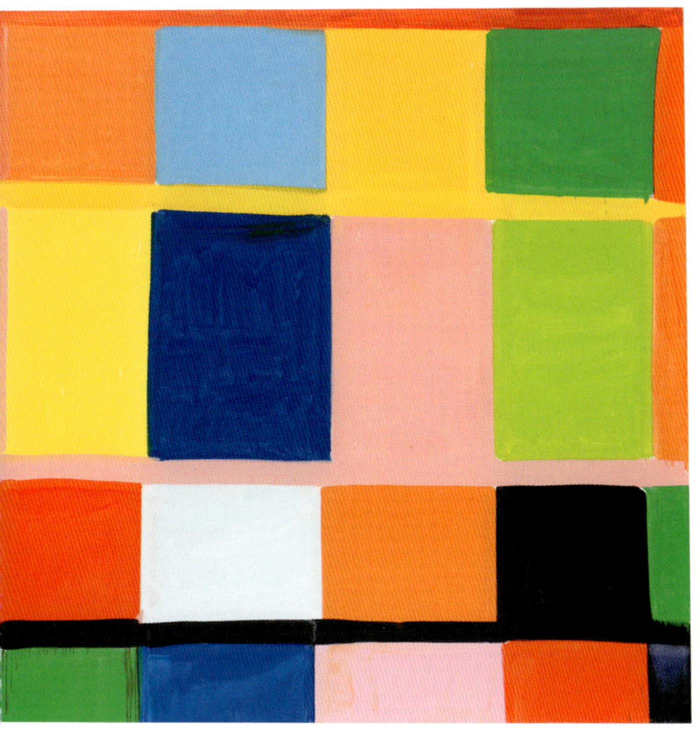

Stanley Whitney
Peaches, 2023
Oil on linen
96 x 96 inches (243.8 x 243.8 cm)

Esther Mahlangu and Alma Thomas

Alma Thomas (1891–1978), an African American painter and a leading figure in the Washington Color School, is celebrated for vibrant abstract paintings that often drew inspiration from nature and the cosmos. The spatial dynamics in Mahlangu's and Thomas's practices reveal a shared knowledge of how color and pattern can transform the viewer's reading of their artwork. Thomas's use of mosaic-like brushstrokes creates a sense of motion and cadence that energizes the pictorial plane, turning it into an abstracted natural world. Similarly, Mahlangu's paintings bring a rhythmic vitality to their surfaces, using color and geometry to redefine their spaces. Both artists recognize that the pictorial plane is a physical realm that can be activated, animated, and filled with energy. Their respective works challenge the viewer to engage with their surroundings differently, demonstrating that abstraction is not only about the forms within the composition but also how they interact with and transform the environment around them.

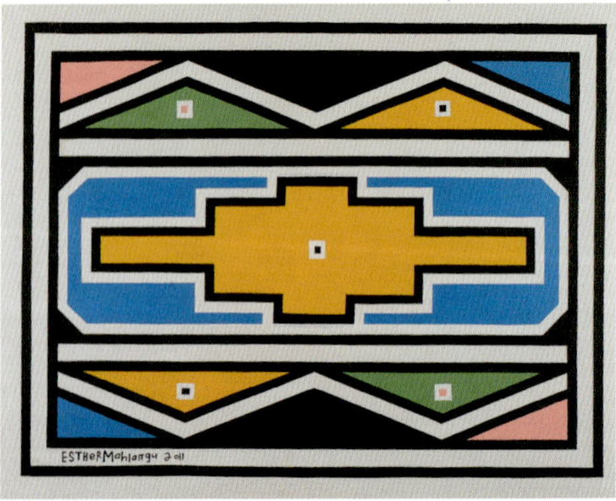

Untitled (Ndebele Abstract), 2011
Acrylic paint on canvas
35 x 47 1/4 inches (90 x 120 cm)

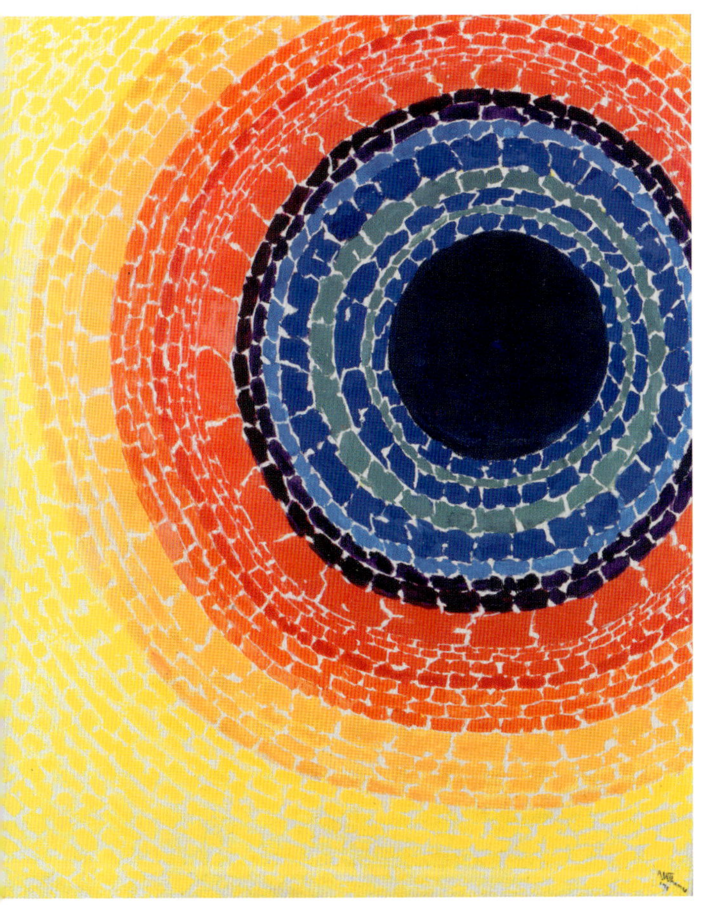

Alma Thomas
The Eclipse, 1970
Acrylic paint on canvas
62 x 49 ³/₄ inches (57.5 x 126.5 cm)

Esther Mahlangu and Lygia Clark

Lygia Clark (1920–1988) was a pioneering Brazilian artist and a central figure in the Neo-Concrete movement. She is known for her innovative explorations of the relationship between art and the viewer. Her work moves beyond traditional art forms, focusing on sensory experiences and participatory engagement to challenge the boundaries of modernist abstraction.

Though entrenched in distinct cultural traditions, Mahlangu and Clark reframe the interaction between art, surface, and audience. Clark creates interactive works, like her *Bichos* series, which invite viewers to engage physically and sensorially with the art, transforming them into active participants. Similarly, Mahlangu's vibrant murals and diverse studio works transform various surfaces—from the walls of Ndebele homes to canvases, ceramics, and vodka bottles—into dynamic stories that resonate locally

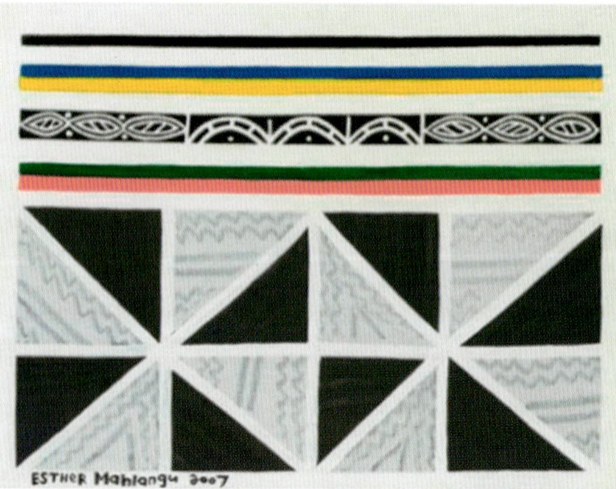

Ndebele Patterns, 2007
Acrylic paint on canvas
23 ⁵/₈ x 31 ¹/₂ inches (60 x 80 cm)

and globally. While Clark breaks down the barriers between artwork and observer through tactile participation, Mahlangu interprets her rich heritage in contemporary mediums, ensuring that her art remains traditional and innovatively relevant. Both artists redefine the role of the creator, using their unique approaches to foster meaningful connections and cultural dialogue across different spaces and audiences.

In juxtaposing Mahlangu's work with these artists, we uncover a rich conversation that transcends the boundaries of culture, geography, and heritage. Mahlangu emerges as a powerful voice within the global narrative of abstraction, challenging and expanding a canon typically dominated by Western perspectives. These comparisons highlight the universality of geometric abstraction and emphasize how deeply interconnected artistic practices can be, regardless of their origins. Like Clark, who redefined the relationship between art and viewer through her participatory works, Mahlangu bridges traditional and contemporary forms, demonstrating that abstraction is a shared language with diverse and vibrant expressions worldwide.

Lygia Clark
Espaço Modulado, No. 10,1958
Automotive paint on wood
35 x 11 ³/₄ x 1 inches (90 x 30 x 3 cm)

Endnote
1. Susan Delson, "Remixing Native American Art," *Wall Street Journal*, February 6, 2020, C14.

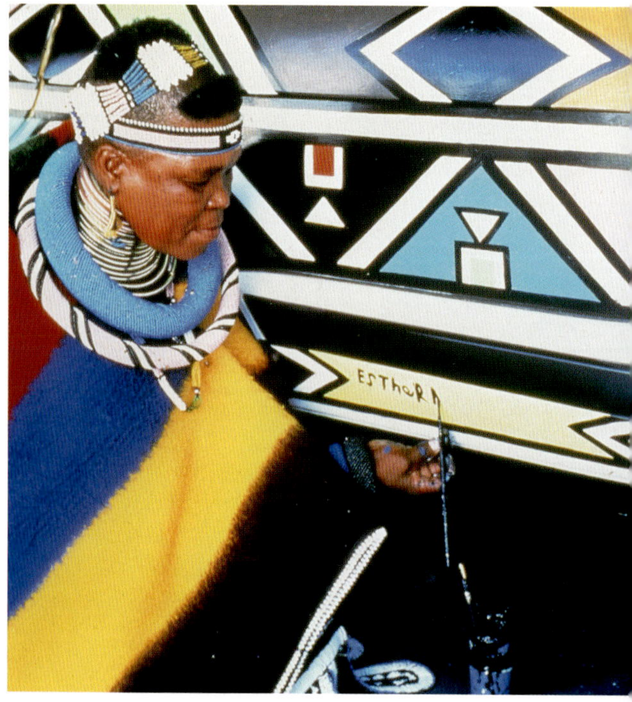

Esther Mahlangu signing her first BMW Art Car, 1991

"Esther Mahlangu's art is like a soulful melody—rich, deep, and profoundly moving. Her patterns and colors resonate with history and culture, yet they feel timeless and universal. Every piece she creates is a powerful testament to the beauty and strength of tradition."

John Legend
Musician and Composer

A CULTURAL ICON

Mahlangu's early work, ingrained in traditional practices, captivated local audiences with its vibrancy and authenticity. This dedication to her heritage laid the groundwork for her becoming a symbol of cultural preservation, and her ability to innovate within the framework of tradition has played a crucial role in her increasing prominence. By sharing the stories behind her work, she has connected with people from many backgrounds, creating a sense of humanity and mutual understanding.

Since first coming to international attention in *Magiciens de la Terre*, Mahlangu's art has been presented in cultural institutions and other prestigious venues worldwide. One of her most notable early collaborations was with the German automaker BMW; in 1991, she became the first woman, African, and non-Western artist to paint a BMW Art Car. (Other BMW Art Car creators have included such art-world luminaries as Andy Warhol, David Hockney, and Frank Stella.) Mahlangu's transformation of the luxury vehicle into a mobile work of art was celebrated for its bold originality and cultural significance, garnering widespread media attention and solidifying her status as an innovative artist. "I painted the car like a wall," she later recalled. "And for the Ndebele people, if you begin to paint a wall, you're announcing either a wedding or a celebration."[1] Mahlangu's participation in this project was her announcement to the international art community that she had arrived. The

BMW model Mahlangu painted—the 525i—also spoke directly to the Black community in South Africa, where the 525i was especially admired. Her work with it was seen as an example of *mkokotelo*, the idea of putting things together and making something new. Still widely exhibited internationally, Mahlangu's 1991 BMW Art Car project—and her BMW AI-and-digital Art Car of 2024—highlight her ability to merge traditional techniques with contemporary and cutting-edge mediums.

From the 2000 Lyon Biennial in France, where her art was presented in conversation with the work of acclaimed conceptual and minimalist artist Sol LeWitt, to a full-building mural on the façade of the National Museum of Women in the Arts in Washington, DC, in 1994, Mahlangu has been showcased in many respected institutions. Her impact is further evidenced by her collaborations with global brands and institutions, bringing her art into popular culture and everyday life.

In recent years, Mahlangu has collaborated with brands like Belvedere Vodka and Nike. Through these collaborations, she extends awareness of her artistic practice, making it accessible to wider audiences. Her striking patterns, vibrant colors, and ability to transcend cultural and linguistic barriers have

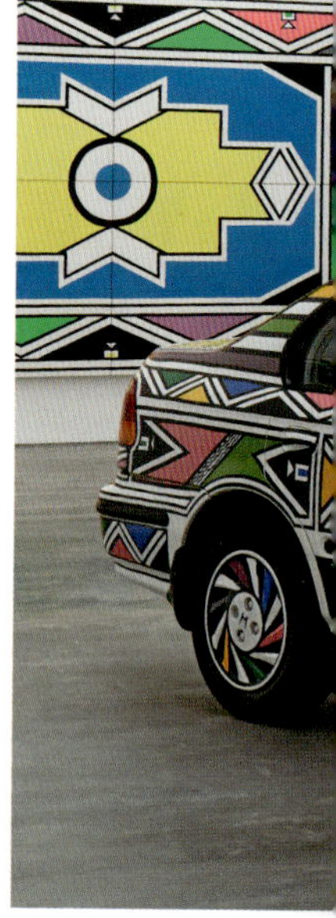

Untitled (Art Car), 2017
1998 Honda Ballade S04, acrylic paint

established her as an international artist and an ambassador of Ndebele culture worldwide.

Mahlangu's art has also earned her institutional accolades. In 2016, the French government honored her with the prestigious *Officier des Arts et des Lettres* (Officer of Arts and Letters). The South African Presidential Order of Ikhamanga and four honorary doctorates from South African universities attest to Mahlangu's cultural contributions to her native country.

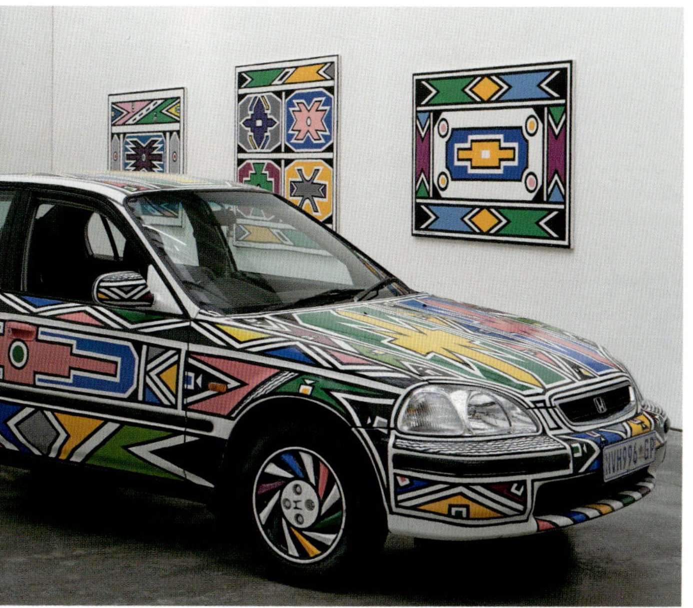

Endnote

1. Exhibition text for *Then I Knew I Was Good at Painting: Esther Mahlangu, A Retrospective*, curated by Nontobeko Ntombela and presented at the Iziko South African National Gallery, Cape Town, and the Wits Art Museum, Johannesburg.

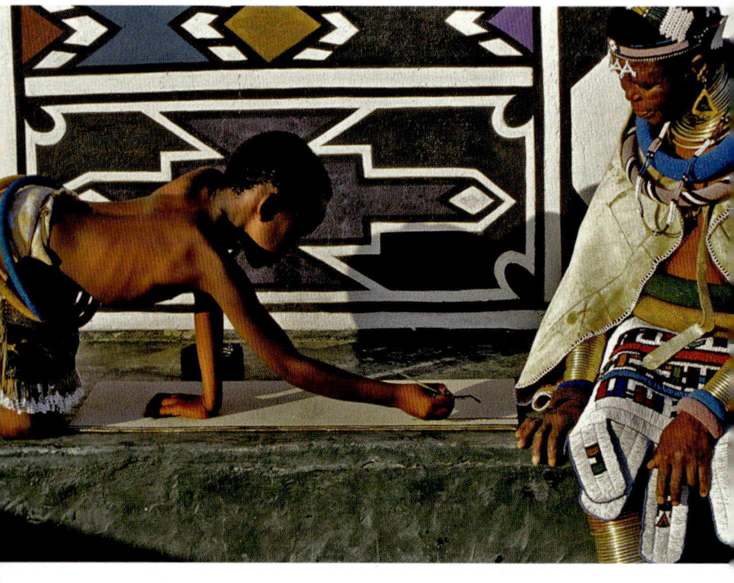

Mahlangu with a student in Mabhoko, Mpumalanga, South Africa, 1992

GIVING BACK

Esther Mahlangu's dedication to giving back shines through her artistic achievements, reflecting a profound commitment to cultural preservation and community uplift. As a mentor and educator, Mahlangu has created workshops and training programs to pass on Ndebele painting and beadwork techniques to younger generations. These initiatives involve more than just the transmission of skills; they are vital to sustaining her community's rich cultural heritage, allowing its young people to learn directly from a living legend. "In my school, I teach not only the Ndebele art form but also the language and cultural aspects, along with the origins of the Ndebele people,"[1] she explains. "You cannot separate the art from the language, culture, and the people because this is where it came from."[2]

Mahlangu's philanthropic efforts also include collaborations with international organizations and institutions. She has partnered with various global entities to support initiatives she deems essential. By leveraging her fame and influence, Mahlangu helps generate resources for crucial causes and promotes the value of art in supporting community wellbeing. These collaborations bring international attention to Ndebele art and help cultivate opportunities for creative dialogue and mutual understanding.

Finally, Mahlangu's influence extends to the global art community through her role as a cultural ambassador.

Her international exhibitions and public appearances elevate the profile of Ndebele art and contribute to a broader understanding of its significance. By representing her culture globally, Mahlangu celebrates Ndebele heritage and encourages a more inclusive and diverse appreciation of artistic traditions. Her efforts help ensure that Indigenous art forms receive the recognition they deserve within the context of contemporary art, fostering greater respect and support for cultural diversity worldwide.

Esther Mahlangu's art is a powerful form of resistance through cultural preservation, international recognition, empowerment of future generations, and adaptation and innovation. In a world increasingly dominated by globalized, homogenized culture, where unique cultural expressions can be overshadowed or forgotten, Mahlangu's work ensures that the Ndebele visual language remains vibrant and alive, nourishing her artistic vision. By meticulously maintaining the techniques and motifs passed down from her ancestors, she protects a critical part of her cultural heritage from being irretrievably lost. "I love art. It is part of me, and I can't separate it from who I am," she has said. "I will continue to paint as long as I am able."[3]

Endnotes

1. Exhibition text for *Then I Knew I Was Good at Painting: Esther Mahlangu, A Retrospective*, curated by Nontobeko Ntombela and presented at the Iziko South African National Gallery, Cape Town, and the Wits Art Museum, Johannesburg.
2. Zaza Hlalethwa, "Mahlangu leads by example," *Mail & Guardian*, Johannesburg, May 18, 2018.
3. "5 life lessons we've learnt from Esther Mahlangu," *S Mag–Sowetan-LIVE*, November 20, 2021.

"I love art. It is part of me, and I can't separate it from who I am. I will continue to paint as long as I am able."

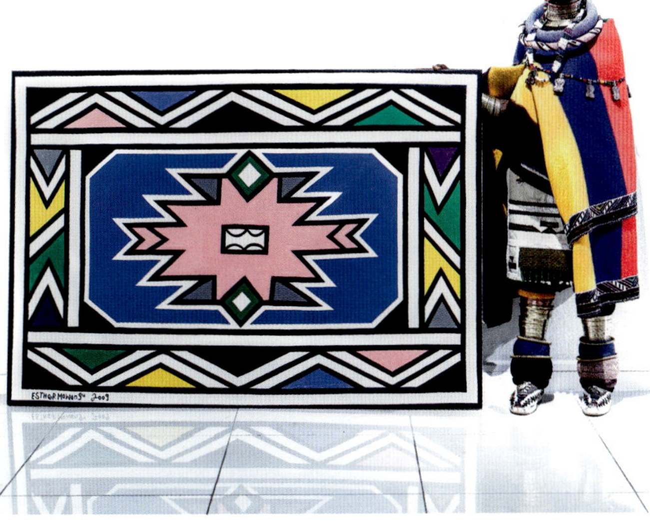

Esther Mahlangu with one of her paintings on canvas,
The Melrose Gallery, Johannesburg, South Africa, 2017

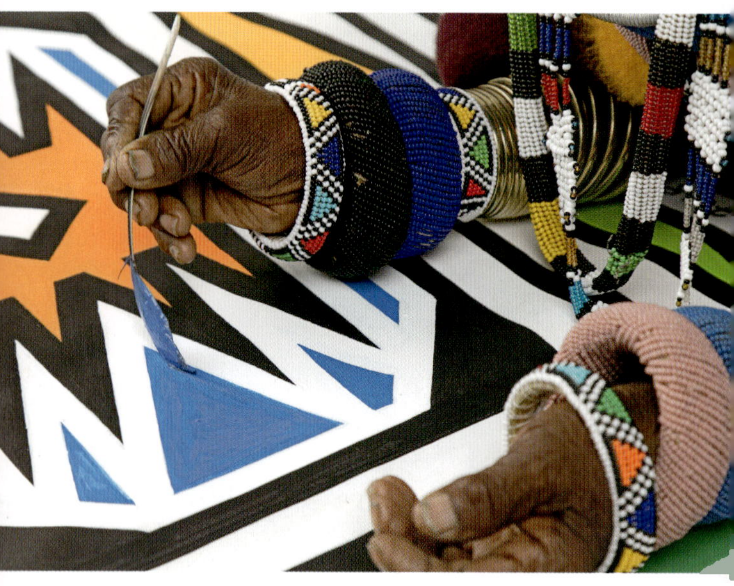

Using a feather as her paintbrush, Mahlangu achieves the sharp-edged shapes that define her abstract geometries. Mpumalanga, South Africa, 2018

CHRONOLOGY

1935

Esther Mahlangu is born in Middelburg, Mpumalanga, South Africa, on November 11.

1945–1946

Mahlangu begins painting her family's home, practicing at first on the back wall, out of public view. This milestone marks a significant moment, signaling Mahlangu's entry into the artistic traditions of her Ndebele community. Under the guidance of the women in her family, she begins to master the intricate geometric patterns that define Ndebele house painting. Traditionally passed down from one generation of Ndebele women to the next, these skills lay the foundation for Mahlangu's groundbreaking contributions to art in the years to come.

1980–1992

Mahlangu begins working at the Botshabelo Historical Village, an open-air museum dedicated to preserving and educating visitors about Ndebele culture. At Botshabelo, Mahlangu demonstrates traditional Ndebele house painting and beadwork. This position allows her to connect with visitors worldwide, planting the seeds for her future role as a global ambassador of Ndebele culture.

1989

Mahlangu participates in *Magiciens de la Terre* at the Centre Georges Pompidou, Paris, France. The landmark exhibition brings together 100 artists from around the world. Half of the artists hail from non-Western countries, challenging the prevailing Eurocentric perspectives of the art world. Her participation in *Magiciens de la Terre* catapults Mahlangu into the global contemporary art world.

Mahlangu is commissioned to create a mural for the Musée des Beaux-Arts in Angoulême, France. As one of her early international engagements, the project further establishes Mahlangu as a pioneering figure in the global art scene.

1991

Mahlangu becomes the first woman and first African artist commissioned to design a BMW Art Car. She transforms the car with bold Ndebele-inspired geometric patterns.

Mahlangu participates in *Ny Afrikansk Billedkunst* (New African Art), a group exhibition presented in Copenhagen, Denmark, from July 6 to August 4. Organized by French curator André Magnin, the exhibition is part of the Images of Africa festival. Other artists in the exhibition include Beninese sculptor and painter Cyprien Tokoudagba, Democratic Republic of Congo artists Cheik Ledy and Moke, and Nigerian artist Emmanuel Ekong Ekefre.

1992

Mahlangu participates in *Africa Hoy* (Africa Now), a traveling exhibition curated by André Magnin that showcases works from the Jean Pigozzi African Art Collection. The exhibition, which features fifteen

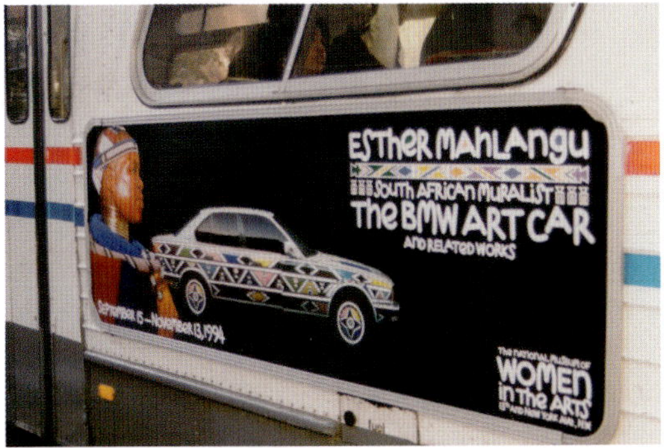

artists living in Africa, debuts in the Canary Islands and tours institutions in the Netherlands and Mexico.

Reconfigured as *Out of Africa*, the *Africa Now* exhibition is presented later that year at the Saatchi Gallery in London. Of eleven artists in this exhibition, Mahlangu is the only woman.

Esther Mahlangu's 1991 BMW 525i Art Car is featured in Documenta 9 in Kassel, Germany. Her participation in this international art event further solidifies her role as a trailblazer in contemporary art and a prominent figure in cross-cultural artistic exchanges.

1994

The exhibition *Out of Africa* travels to the Musée des Beaux-Arts de Nantes, France.

At the National Museum of Women in the Arts (NMWA) in Washington, DC, Mahlangu creates a mural on the façade of the museum's new annex. She is the first artist com-

An ad on a Washington, DC, bus announces the exhibition *Esther Mahlangu, South African Muralist: The BMW Art Car and Related Works*, presented by the National Museum of Women in the Arts, 1994

missioned for such a project at the museum. This mural is a centerpiece of the exhibition *Esther Mahlangu, South African Muralist: The BMW Art Car and Related Works*.

1995

Mahlangu participates in *Africus*, the first Johannesburg Biennale, held February 28–April 30.

Her work is included in the exhibition *Eight From South Africa*, presented at the Yerba Buena Center for the Arts, San Francisco.

1999

Mahlangu participates in *<<Rewind>>Fast Forward. ZA: New Work from South Africa*, presented at the Van Reekum Museum, Apeldoorn, Netherlands. Other artists in the exhibition include William Kentridge, Zwelethu Mthethwa, Willie Bester, Kevin Brand, Bongiwe Dhlomo-Mautloa, Noria Mabasa, Sam Nhlengethwa, Nikosana Dominic Tschabangu, and Sue Williamson.

2000

Mahlangu participates in *Partage d'Exotismes*, presented at the 5th Biennale of Contemporary Art in Lyon, France. The exhibition explores global artistic exchanges and the concept of "exoticism" in contemporary art. Mahlangu's work is presented in conversation with the work of American conceptual artist Sol LeWitt, highlighting the intersections between her vibrant, culturally rich designs and LeWitt's minimalist geometric forms.

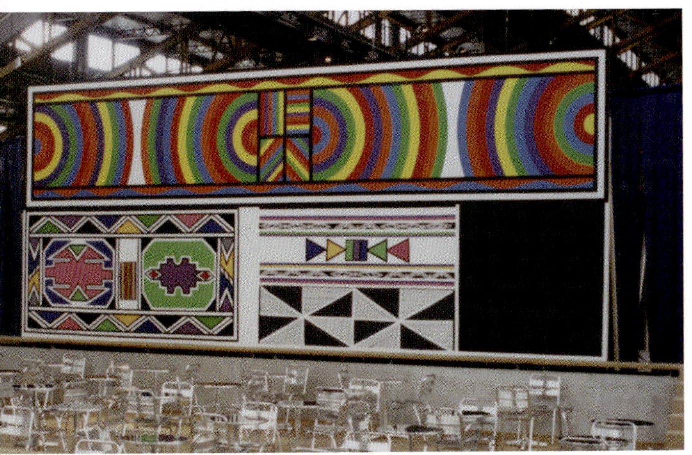

2001

Mahlangu's art is included in the exhibition *South Africa Today*, presented at the Helsinki Fair Center, Helsinki Finland.

2004

Mahlangu collaborates with Nelson Mandela on a special project. In 2002, Mandela revisits Robben Island and creates a series of evocative sketches—depicting a clenched fist, chained hands, and hands breaking free—that reflect his imprisonment there. Mahlangu responds to these drawings by adding her signature geometric and figurative patterns, creating a powerful dialogue between their personal histories and artistic languages.

Mahlangu executes a 78-foot-long mural at the Bochum Art Museum in Bochum, Germany, as part of the *New Identities: Contemporary South African Art* exhibition.

Esther Mahlangu, **U'gwala**, 2000, presented in dialogue with Sol LeWitt, **Wall Work #947** at the 5th Lyon Biennial, Lyon, France, 2000

2005

Mahlangu participates in *African Art Now*, a group show exploring the dynamic landscape of contemporary art across sub-Saharan Africa. The exhibition, which is presented at the Smithsonian in Washington, DC, and the Museum of Fine Arts Houston, in Texas, showcases the work of leading painters, photographers, sculptors, and installation artists from nineteen countries, including Angola, South Africa, Tanzania, and Togo. It examines how these artists engage with their cultural heritage while embracing contemporary global dialogues, forging multifaceted artistic identities that challenge conventional narratives of African creativity.

Mahlangu is part of *New Identities – Contemporary Art from South Africa*. A group exhibition presented at the Pretoria Art Museum and Johannesburg Art Gallery, it reflects on the end of Apartheid in South Africa and the first free elections in 1994. The exhibition examines how visual art played an instrumental role in societal change and how the quest for national identity is vividly reflected in its diversity. Highlighting the work of seventeen artists at the forefront of South Africa's contemporary art scene, the exhibition presents traditional forms of artistic expression, such as Ndebele murals and sculptural drums, on an equal footing with contemporary works such as installations and videos.

Mahlangu completes an artist residency at Project Row Houses, the art- and community-centered organization based in the Houston, Texas, Third Ward neighborhood. Organized around a core of several traditional southern "shotgun houses"—so called because the house's front and back doors are aligned, so that shooting a shotgun through the house would not hit any walls—Project Row Houses presents two rounds of artists' installations per year. A participant in the 22nd round, Mahlangu creates a dynamic interplay between her art and the traditional shotgun-house architecture.

2006

Mahlangu's art is included in *100% African: The Jean Pigozzi Contemporary African Art Collection,* presented at the Guggenheim Museum in Bilbao, Spain, from October 12, 2006, to February 18, 2007.

The government of South Africa presents Mahlangu with the Order of Ikhamanga (Silver), which recognizes outstanding achievements in arts, culture, literature, music, journalism, and sports.

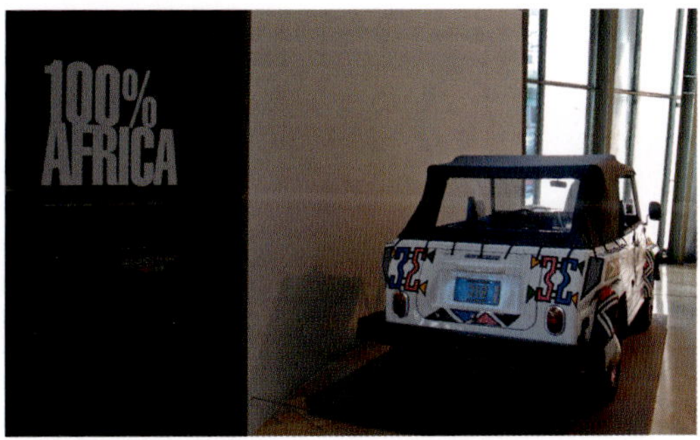

A Mahlangu art car is one of the signature works in *100% African: The Jean Pigozzi Contemporary African Art Collection* at the Guggenheim Bilbao

2007

Mahlangu is featured in the group exhibition *Why Africa?* Presented at the Pinacoteca Giovanni e Marella Agnelli in Turin, Italy, the exhibition showcases the work of several African artists.

2009

Mahlangu's work is featured in *Against Exclusion*, the central exhibition of the 3rd Moscow Biennale, presented in Moscow, Russian Federation, September 24–November 1, 2009. Curated by Jean-Hubert Martin, the exhibition expands the cross-cultural conversation by juxtaposing the work of well-known Western artists with non-Western and nonprofessional artists.

2010

Mahlangu is chosen as a FIFA Official Artist for South Africa.

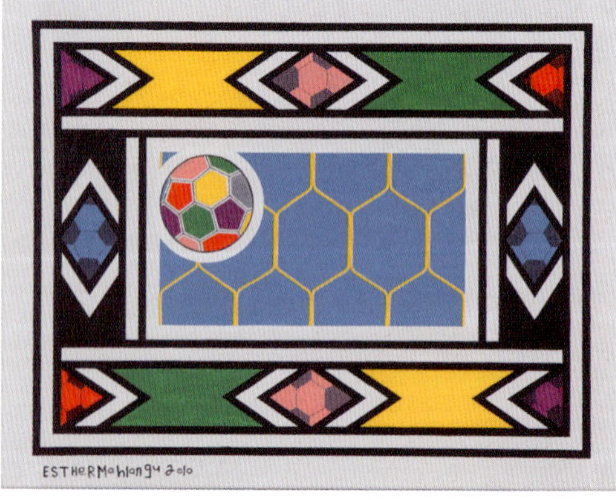

2010 FIFA World Cup, 2010
Acrylic paint on canvas
28 x 35 inches (70 x 90 cm)

Mahlangu's 1991 BMW Art Car is featured in the *Global Africa Project* exhibition at the Museum of Art and Design in New York City, on view from November 17, 2010, to May 15, 2011.

2014

At the age of 78, Mahlangu is commissioned by the Virginia Museum of Fine Arts in Richmond, Virginia, to create two large murals for the entrance to its African art galleries. During a month-long residency, visitors watch Mahlangu and her granddaughter, Marriam, paint two 9-by-15-foot murals inspired by Ndebele art. Mahlangu also teaches art classes for children, a practice she regularly engages in at her studio and home in South Africa.

2016

Mahlangu collaborates with Grammy and Oscar-winning composer and musician John Legend to create an Ndebele-inspired design for a special-edition bottle of Belvedere (Red) vodka. A significant percentage of the profits are contributed to the Global Fund, a leading resource for HIV/AIDS prevention in Africa.

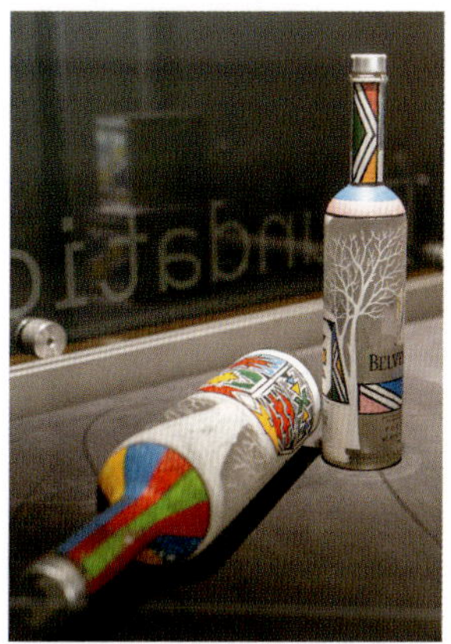

Two versions of the special edition Belvedere (Red) Vodka bottle designed in 2016 by Mahlangu in collaboration with John Legend, shown in the exhibition *Then I Knew I Was Good at Painting: Esther Mahlangu, A Retrospective*, curated by Nontobeko Ntombela and presented at the Iziko South African National Gallery, Cape Town, and the Wits Art Museum in Johannesburg

2018

Mahlangu receives an honorary doctorate from the Durban University of Technology, Durban, South Africa.

She receives an honorary doctorate from the University of Johannesburg, Johannesburg, South Africa.

2019

The government of France appoints Mahlangu as an Officer of Arts and Letters, one of the country's highest honors, for her contribution to the arts.

The South African Department of Arts and Culture publishes a book about Mahlangu and her art as part of its launch of Women's Month 2019.

Mahlangu receives the first United Nations—South Africa HCR Award for her efforts to promote inclusivity and empowerment in South Africa.

2020

The exhibition *Esther Mahlangu 85*, presented at the Melrose Gallery in Johannesburg, South Africa, show-cases her art and its decades-long evolution.

The exhibition *Dr. Esther Mahlangu—Disrupting Patterns*, shown at the Melrose Gallery in Cape Town, South Africa, underscores her ongoing influence and legacy.

Mahlangu is commissioned by a South African patron

to create one-of-a-kind art for a Rolls-Royce dubbed "The Mahlangu Phantom," which displays the art under glass in a dashboard gallery.

2021

Dr. Esther Mahlangu, an exhibition at Almine Rech Gallery in Paris, showcases paintings created between 2019 and 2021. It runs from November 20 to December 11.

2023

The solo exhibition *Dr. Esther Mahlangu* opens April 15 at Almine Rech Gallery, Paris, where it runs through June 3. On April 20, *Dr. Esther Mahlangu: Where two rivers meet* opens at Almine Rech Gallery, London, continuing through May 20.

Opening April 21, *Dr. Esther Mahlangu: The Breath of Calligraphy* presents a selection of acrylic paintings made between 2010 and 2022 at the Enrico Navarra Gallery in Paris. Presented with Almine Rech Gallery, the exhibition runs through June 30.

Mahlangu's work is prominently featured in *Africa Fashion* at the Brooklyn Museum in Brooklyn, New York. Organized by Ernestine White-Mifetu and Annissa Malvoisin with Catherine Futter, Matthew Yokobosky, and Rhea Stark, the exhibition celebrates African fashion's creativity, global impact, and cultural significance. Mahlangu's iconic designs are presented alongside works by African designers and artists, highlighting the exchanges between art, fashion, and identity.

2024

In January, Mahlangu's work is featured in *Sisters of the Desert*, a key project of Dhai Dubai, the first Dubai Light Festival, held in Dubai, United Arab Emirates. Projecting Mahlangu's signature patterns in a dynamic, illuminated environment, the installation brings her geometric designs to life in an immersive, global context.

Mahlangu's art is included in the exhibition *GIANTS: Art from the Dean Collection of Swizz Beatz and Alicia Keys*, on view at the Brooklyn Museum. Curated by Kimberli Gant and Indira A. Abiskaroon, the exhibition runs February 10–July 7. It then travels to the High Museum of Art in Atlanta, Georgia, running September 13, 2024–January 19, 2025. It subsequently runs at the Minneapolis Institute of Art from March 8th to July 13th, 2025.

In February, Mahlangu's new Art Car, the BMW i5 *Flow Nostokana*, debuts at the Frieze art fair in Los Angeles. With its surfaces covered in film that can be electronically animated, the *Nostokana* features dynamic presentations of Mahlangu's art, developed using AI.

Mahlangu's art is included in *Stranieri Ovunque–Foreigners Everywhere*, the central project of the 60th International Venice Biennale. Curated by Adriano Pedrosa, the

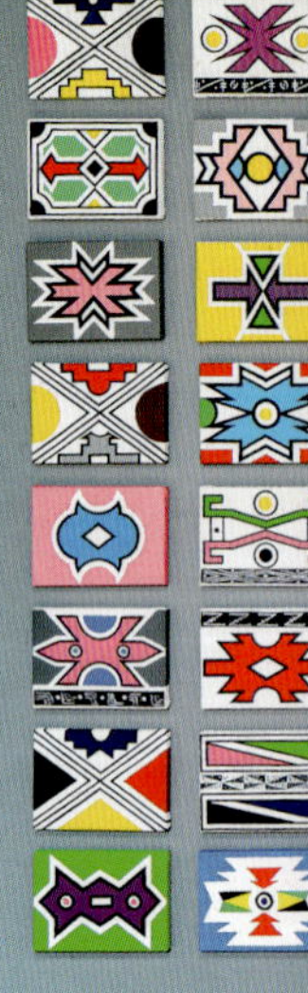

exhibition explores themes of foreignness, displacement, and the fluidity of identity. The Biennale runs
April 20–November 24.

The solo exhibition *Dr. Esther Mahlangu: The Order of
Things* opens on June 7 at Almine Rech Gallery in Paris
and runs through July 20.

The exhibition *Then I Knew I Was Good at Painting:
Esther Mahlangu, A Retrospective*, curated by Nonto-
beko Ntombela, opens at the Iziko National Gallery in
Cape Town, South Africa. On view from February 18 to
August 11, it features over 100 contemporary artworks,

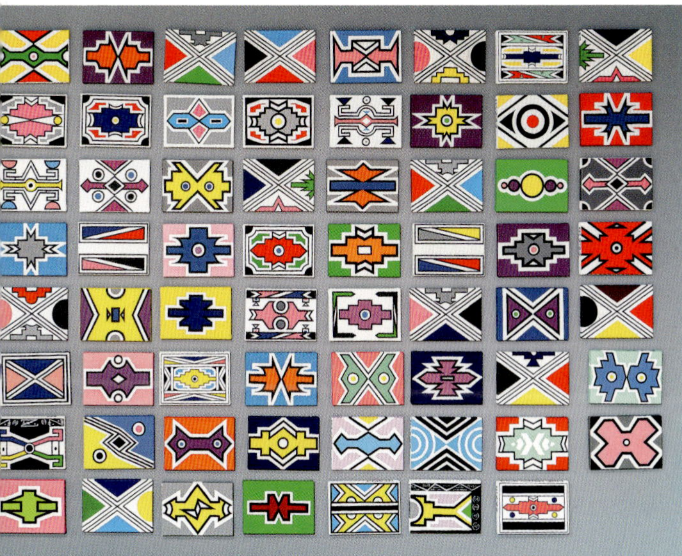

87 Gestures, 2022
Acrylic paint on canvas
87 works: 8 x 11 ¾ inches (20 x 30 cm) each

historic photographs, and a short film. The exhibition then moves to the Wits Art Museum in Johannesburg, South Africa, where it remains on view from November 20, 2024, through April 17, 2025.

The Serpentine Gallery, London, presents the artist's first public mural in the UK. Sited in the garden of Serpentine North, the mural is painted on sixteen wooden panels. It depicts Ndebele motifs outlined with black borders. The title, *Umuntu ngumuntu ngabantu*, translates as "I am because you are," emphasizing the importance of communities and unity among humans and other living species.

In New York's Chelsea gallery district, *Esther Mahlangu: Time in Color* opens November 21 at Ross + Kramer Gallery, where it runs through January 25, 2025. The solo exhibition features more than 30 works created between 2011 and 2021.

2025

Mahlangu participates in *Kings and Queens of Africa: Forms and Figures of Power,* on view at the Louvre Abu Dhabi from January 29th to May 25th. Curated by Hélène Joubert, El Hadji Malick Ndiaye, and Cindy Olohou, the exhibition presents more than 350 works from all parts of the continent. At night, Mahlangu's *Projection of Harmony* illuminates the museum's architecture with her signature geometric patterns.

Architect Francis Kéré, Creative Director, Nachson Mimran, and Swiss architects Chaletbau Matti commission Esther Mahlangu to create a series of large-scale murals for a private residence in Gstaad that showcases art and design from Africa and the African Diaspora.

When Heart and Mind Agree, a solo exhibition of paintings and sculptures by Esther Mahlangu, is presented at Jenkins Johnson Gallery, San Francisco. Running March 15–May 3, it is Mahlangu's first solo exhibition on the West Coast of the United States.

Mahlangu is among the close to 40 international artists included in the exhibition *FEMMES* at Perrotin Gallery, Paris. Curated by singer, songwriter, musician, music producer, and fashion designer Pharrell Williams for Perrotin Gallery, Paris, the exhibition runs March 20–April 19.

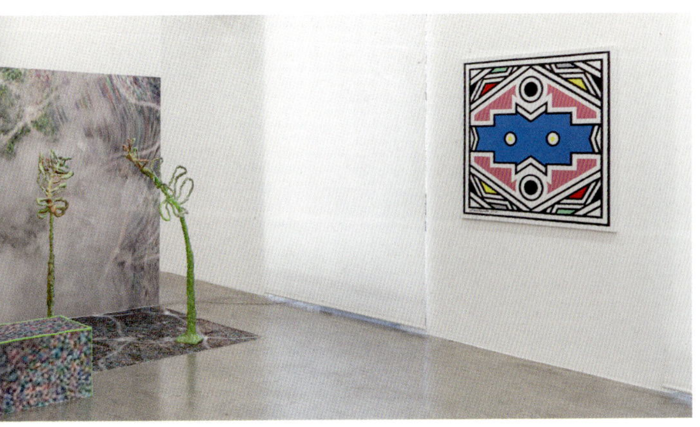

Mahlangu's art presented in the exhibition *FEMMES* at Perrotin Gallery, Paris, in 2025

CREDITS

Artworks

Front cover: Property of Rita and Craig Hollingworth, The Hollingworth Collection

Pages 28–29, 41 (below), 94, 96, 100, 120: Collection of Larry Warsh

Pages 40, 41 (above), 46–47, 48, 49, 51 (left and right), 57 (left), 98: Private Collection

Pages 42–43, 124–125: Collection of Benjamin Milstein / The Melrose Gallery

Pages 44, 45: Collection of the artist / The Melrose Gallery

Page 102: Jorge M. Pérez Collection

Photography

Pages 4, 24, 26–27, 38–39: Photograph by David Stover. Courtesy Virginia Museum of Fine Arts Photo Archive. © Virginia Museum of Fine Arts

Pages 8, 17, 36–37, 60–61, 108: © M. Courtney-Clarke

Page 10: Courtesy Iziko South African National Gallery / The Melrose Gallery

Pages 11, 12–13, 14, 15, 18, 19, 32, 33, 34–35, 58, 111, 112: Photograph by Clint Strydom. Courtesy Clint Strydom / The Melrose Gallery

Pages 22–23: Photograph by Béatrice Hatala, Konstantinos Ignatiadis. © CNAC/MNAN, Dist. RMN-Grand Palais / Art Resource, NY

Pages 30–31, 84, 85: Photograph by Nicolas Brasseur. Courtesy the artist and Almine Rech

Pages 42–43, 55 (above and below), 57 (above and below), 71, 72, 73, 121, 124–125: Courtesy The Melrose Gallery

Pages 46–47, 48, 49, 91, 106–107: Photograph by Grace Dodds. Courtesy Ross + Kramer, New York

Pages 53, 78, 134: Photograph by Bill Fitz-Patrick. Courtesy National Museum of Women in the Arts, Betty Boyd Dettre Library and Research Center. © Dr. Esther Mahlangu

Pages 62–63: Photograph by Richard Woodward. Courtesy Virginia Museum of Fine Arts Photo Archive. © Virginia Museum of Fine Arts

Pages 64–65: Courtesy BMW

Pages 66–67: Courtesy Dhai Dubai 2024, co-curated by AGB
Creative & Expo City Dubai

Pages 68–69 (above and below): Photograph by Daryll Borja –
Seeing Things. © Department of Culture and Tourism, Abu Dhabi

Pages 74–75: Photograph by George Darrell. Courtesy Serpentine
Gallery / The Melrose Gallery

Pages 76–77, 93: Photograph by Wim Starkenburg. Courtesy Estate
of Sol LeWitt

Pages 80, 81, 82, 83: Courtesy Farida and Henri Seydoux
Collection. © Filipe Santo

Pages 86–87: Photograph by Cecil Mathieu. Courtesy Nachson
Mimran

Page 88: Photograph by Melissa Castro Duarte. Courtesy the artist
and Almine Rech

Page 95: Photograph by Adam Reich. Courtesy Lisson Gallery.
© Carmen Herrera

Page 97: Photograph by Max Yawny. Courtesy the artist and
Hauser & Wirth. © Jeffrey Gibson

Page 99: Photograph by Robert McKeever. Courtesy Stanley
Whitney Studio and Gagosian Gallery

Page 101: Courtesy Smithsonian American Art Museum,
Washington, DC / Art Resource, NY © ARS, NY

Page 102: Courtesy Jorge M. Pérez Collection

Page 103: Photograph by Mario da Costa Grisolli. Courtesy "The
World of Lygia Clark" Cultural Association

Pages 104, 115: Courtesy National Museum of Women in the Arts,
Betty Boyd Dettre Library and Research Center. © Dr. Esther
Mahlangu

Page 117: © Blaise Adilon

Page 119: Courtesy the Guggenheim Museum

Page 127: Photograph by Claire Dorn. Courtesy Perrotin Gallery

ACKNOWLEDGMENTS

Above all, my deepest gratitude goes to Dr. Esther Mahlangu, whose extraordinary life and groundbreaking work have served as the foundation of this project. I am in awe of her creative vision, depth of spirit, and immense talent. My heartfelt thanks also to Betty and Musa Mahlangu for their invaluable support.

I am sincerely thankful to curator Larry Ossei-Mensah for the research and authorship that are the cornerstone of this publication. Larry has a keen appreciation of Mahlangu and her achievements as a global contemporary artist. His insights, vision, and scholarship have been essential in introducing her work to new audiences with the *Esther Mahlangu Handbook*, and I am grateful for his collaboration.

I am especially grateful to Craig Mark, Clint Strydom, and the dedicated team at the Melrose Gallery—Dr. Mahlangu's exclusive global representative—for their steadfast support.

My deep appreciation also goes to Nontobeko Ntombela for her masterful organization and curatorial direction of the powerful exhibition *Then I Knew I Was Good at Painting: Esther Mahlangu, A Retrospective*. Her scholarship has made an invaluable contribution to the study of Dr. Mahlangu's art. I am also thankful to the exceptional teams at the

Iziko South African National Gallery and the Wits Art Museum in Johannesburg for bringing this landmark retrospective to life.

My thanks as well to all who have championed and supported Dr. Mahlangu's work. Individuals and institutions include the American Federation of the Arts; Dr. Thomas Girst and Eduard Weidenhammer at BMW; Ann Pasternak, Sharon Matt Atkins, and Ernestine White-Mifetu at the Brooklyn Museum; Melissa Chu at the Hirshhorn Museum and Sculpture Garden; the Lyon Biennale; the National Museum of Women in the Arts; Franklin Sirmans at the Pérez Art Museum Miami; the Jorge M. Pérez Collection; and the Virginia Museum of Fine Arts. Among galleries and gallerists, my thanks to Almine Rech Gallery; Lucas and Esteban Jaramillo at Galería La Cometa; Doriano Navarra at Galerie Enrico Navarra; Karen Jenkins Johnson and the Jenkins Johnson Gallery; and Ross + Kramer Gallery.

I am grateful, too, to individuals who have supported Dr. Mahlangu's work and in many cases, the work of bringing her art to broader audiences. Among them are Swizz Beatz, Mike Dean, Ralph DeLuca, Louise Donegan, Howard and Pat Farber, Brian Frasca, Tom Hardy, Paul Henkle, Zara Hoffman, Craig Hollingsworth, Man Huang, CJ Jones, Alicia Keys, Karen Lautanen, John Legend, Agnes Lew, Benjamin Milstein, Jasmine Mueller, Danny O'Neill,

Bojana Popovic, David and Lori Reservitz, Jean Rim, Leslie Russo, Hassan Smith, Sarah Sperling, Loïc Villepontoux, and Pharrell Williams.

Very special thanks as well to Hans Ulrich Obrist for his unwavering support of Dr. Mahlangu and her work over many years.

Curator Larry Ossei-Mensah would also like to extend his personal gratitude to Esther Mahlangu—a remarkable artistic force whose creativity, wisdom, and generosity of spirit have profoundly expanded his understanding of art and its practice. For Ossei-Mensah, this book is a tribute to Dr. Mahlangu's immense contribution and ongoing influence on contemporary culture. He extends his gratitude as well to Nontobeko Ntombela for her time and insights, and to the following individuals who have been crucial in the process of creating this publication: Anelys Alvarez, Art Resource, Kendall Ayers, Natasha Becker, Kate Seno Bradshaw, Ethan Buchsbaum, Lygia Clark, Margaret Courtney-Clarke, Rhea L. Combs, Joyce Faust, Kimberi Gant, Jeffrey Gibson and his gallery Hauser & Wirth, Johnathan Gardenhire, Fréderique Gautier, Sophia Haaland and Almeida & Dale, Louise Hayward and Lisson Gallery, Carmen Herrera, Karen Jenkins Johnson, Kent Kelley, Kate Kaluzny, Emily Larson, John Legend, Carol LeWitt, Florence Lynch, Chris Lyons, Nelson

Makamo, Craig Marks, The Melrose Gallery, David Mitchell, Azu Nwagbogu, Valerie Cassel Oliver, Daniela Olivero, Ann Patsch, Jorge M. Pérez, Howell Perkins, Hassan Smith, Clint Strydom, Alma Thomas, Virginia (Ginny) Treanor, Ph.D., Ernestine White-Mifetu, Stanley Whitney, and Richard Woodward.

On behalf of the No More Rulers team, our warmest thanks to the entire team at D.A.P., whose partnership has made the *Handbook* series possible, with special appreciation to Brandon Johnson, Stephanie Rebonati, and Maya Perry.

I would also like to express my sincere gratitude to Hannah Alderfer for her exceptional design work; to Susan Delson for her keen editorial guidance; and to Fiona Graham for her vital role in overseeing this and many other publications. I am also grateful to Taliesin Thomas for her meaningful contributions, and to Steven Rodríguez for his indispensable support.

Finally, I thank my wife, Abbey, and my children—Justin, Ethan, Ellie, and Jonah—for their love and unwavering support. And as always, I give my endless love and thanks to my mother Judith.

Larry Warsh
New York City
July 2025

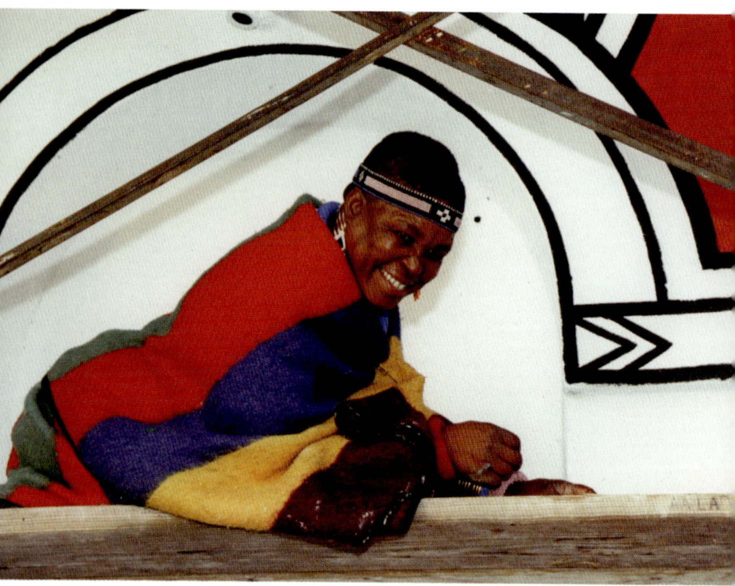

Esther Mahlangu at work on her façade installation at the National Museum of Women in the Arts, Washington, DC, during the exhibition *Esther Mahlangu, South African Muralist: The BMW Art Car and Related Works*, 1994

ESTHER MAHLANGU

Born in 1935 in the rural village of Middelburg, South Africa, Dr. Esther Mahlangu's life and artistic practice have always moved in rhythm—with the painted line, personal heritage, and time. Raised within the visual traditions of the Ndebele people, she began painting at an early age, learning by watching the women in her family transform the walls of their homestead into bold, geometric expressions. These motifs became Mahlangu's first visual language—an early initiation into a broader dialogue around identity, visibility, and cultural resilience.

While her artistry is rooted in this lineage, it has never been bound by it. Mahlangu has expanded the surfaces and contexts of her work, carrying Ndebele aesthetics into unexpected spaces: from gallery walls to the body of a BMW, from canvas to couture.

Her international breakthrough with *Magiciens de la Terre* (1989) at the Centre Pompidou in Paris elevated her to the global contemporary stage. From that pivotal moment to *Kings and Queens of Africa: Forms and Figures of Power* (2025) at the Louvre Abu Dhabi, Mahlangu has charted a singular path—fearless, visionary, and deeply rooted in her people.

LARRY OSSEI-MENSAH

Larry Ossei-Mensah is a Ghanaian-American curator, cultural critic, and global champion of contemporary art whose bold, boundary-breaking practice continues to shape the international art landscape. With projects spanning Manila, London, Athens, São Paulo, Rome, and beyond, his curatorial vision uplifts diverse voices and sparks cross-cultural dialogue.

Ossei-Mensah has collaborated with a powerful roster of artists—including Steve McQueen, Catherine Opie, Judy Chicago, Shinque Smith, Chase Hall, and Sonia Gomes—bringing their work to life through exhibitions at institutions like the Museum of Contemporary Art Detroit (MOCAD), Brooklyn Academy of Music (BAM), MASS MoCA, The MET in Manila, Seattle Art Museum, Denver Art Museum, Museum of the African Diaspora (MOAD) in San Francisco, and Ben Brown Fine Arts in Hong Kong and London, among others.

As co-founder of ARTNOIR, a nonprofit committed to supporting underrepresented artists and curators, Ossei-Mensah continues to reimagine what inclusive cultural leadership looks like. Recent projects such as *The Poetics of Dimensions* at ICA San Francisco and *Sonia Gomes: Ó Abre Alas!* at Storm King (co-curated with Executive Director Nora R. Lawrence) reflect his enduring commitment to creative empowerment and his role as a dynamic force in shaping the future of contemporary art.

LARRY WARSH

Larry Warsh has been active in the art world for more than thirty years as a publisher and artist-collaborator. An early collector of Keith Haring and Jean-Michel Basquiat, Warsh was a lead organizer for the exhibition *Basquiat: The Unknown Notebooks*, which debuted at the Brooklyn Museum, in 2015 and continues to travel to international museums. He has loaned artworks by Haring and Basquiat from his collection to numerous exhibitions worldwide and he served as a curatorial consultant on *Keith Haring | Jean-Michel Basquiat: Crossing Lines* for the National Gallery of Victoria, Melbourne.

In addition to the *Handbook* series, Warsh has edited numerous publishing projects including the Princeton University Press *-isms* series, which includes titles on Basquiat, Haring, Marina Abramović, Jenny Holzer, Judy Chicago, Yoko Ono, Marcel Duchamp, Alexander Calder, and other renowned artists. Warsh was also the editor of *Jean-Michel Basquiat: The Notebooks* (2017), *Keith Haring: 31 Subway Drawings* (2021), *James Rosenquist: Collages, Drawings, and Paintings in Process* (2024), and *Wassily Kandinsky: The Sketchbooks* (2025), all published by Princeton University Press. Warsh was a founding member of the Basquiat Authentication Committee from 1993 until its dissolution in 2012.

NO MORE RULERS (NMR) is on a mission to rethink the way we define art and creative expression. Based in New York, NMR is a publishing company dedicated to empowering the creative community and questioning the status quo. Our artist publications erase the boundaries between high and low, popular culture and fine art, and between traditional categories like design, music, and fashion. By partnering with global institutions and focusing on topics ranging from contemporary culture to artistic process to creativity, we're creating a world where art can truly be for everyone.

NO MORE RULERS